The Power of Self Love

Unlocking Your True Potential through Daily Affirmations

IRENE DITTMAN

© Copyright 2024 by IRENE DITTMAN
All Rights Reserved

The presentation of the information is without contract or any type of guarantee assurance. The trademarks that are used are without any consent, and the publication of the trademark is without permission or backing by the trademark owner. All trademarks and brands within this book are for clarifying purposes only and are the owned by the owners themselves, not affiliated with this document.

Table of Contents

Chapter 1 6

Introduction 6

   The Concept of Self-Love.................................. 6

   The Role of Daily Affirmations........................ 9

   How to Use This Book Effectively 13

   Setting Your Intentions for the Journey 18

   Overview of the Path Ahead 21

Chapter 2 26

The Foundation of Self-Love............................. 26

   Defining Self-Love: What It Is and What It Isn't.. 26

   The Science behind Self-Love......................... 30

   Common Myths and Misconceptions................ 34

   The Benefits of Embracing Self-Love....................37

   Real-Life Transformations through Self-Love.......41

Chapter 3 46

Understanding Affirmations 46

   What Are Affirmations?................................... 46

   The Psychological Impact of Affirmations 50

   How Affirmations Influence Self-Perception........ 54

   Crafting Effective Affirmations 57

   Examples of Powerful Affirmations 61

Chapter 4 66

Creating Your Personal Affirmation Practice 66

   Setting Up a Daily Routine............................... 66

Integrating Affirmations into Your Morning Ritual
.... 70

Using Affirmations throughout the Day 74

Evening Reflections and Affirmations 78

Overcoming Challenges in Maintaining Consistency
.... 82

Chapter 5 86

Affirmations for Building Self-Worth 86

Identifying Areas of Low Self-Worth 86

Affirmations to Boost Self-Esteem 90

Techniques for Reinforcing Positive Self-Image... 94

Real-Life Stories of Enhanced Self-Worth 98

Daily Exercises for Sustained Self-Worth 102

Chapter 1

Introduction

The Concept of Self-Love

Self-love is the cornerstone of a fulfilling and balanced life, yet it is often misunderstood or overlooked. This chapter delves into the essence of self-love, exploring its significance, dispelling common myths, and offering insights into how it can transform your life.

At its core, self-love is an appreciation of oneself that grows from actions that support our physical, psychological, and spiritual growth. It is not about narcissism or self-absorption; rather, it is about valuing yourself as a person who deserves happiness, respect, and compassion. Self-love means having a high regard for your own well-being and happiness, taking care of your own needs, and not sacrificing your well-being to please others.

The journey to self-love often begins with a shift in mindset. Many people grow up internalizing negative messages about themselves, whether from family, society, or personal experiences. These messages can create a self-critical inner voice that undermines our sense of worth. Cultivating self-love involves recognizing and challenging these negative beliefs, replacing them with positive affirmations and a more compassionate self-view.

One of the most significant aspects of self-love is self-compassion. This means being kind and understanding to yourself when confronted with personal failings, rather than being harshly self-critical. Self-compassion involves recognizing that imperfection is part of the human experience, and it allows us to treat ourselves with the same kindness we would offer a friend in a similar situation. This shift in perspective can have profound effects on our mental and emotional well-being.

Another crucial component of self-love is self-care. This involves taking deliberate actions to care for your physical, emotional, and mental health. Self-care can take many forms, from ensuring you get enough sleep and eat nutritious foods to engaging in activities that bring you joy and relaxation. It also means setting boundaries and saying no to things that drain your energy or harm your well-being. By prioritizing self-care, you send a powerful message to yourself that you are worth the effort and attention.

Self-love also requires self-awareness. This means taking the time to understand your own needs, desires, and emotions. It involves being honest with yourself about what you want and need to feel fulfilled. Self-awareness allows you to make choices that align with your true self, rather than making decisions based on external pressures or expectations. This can lead to a more authentic and satisfying life.

One of the barriers to self-love is the prevalence of self-comparison. In a world saturated with social media and curated images of perfection, it is easy to fall into the trap of comparing yourself to others and feeling inadequate. Self-love involves recognizing that everyone's journey is unique and that comparing yourself to others is not only unfair but also unproductive. Instead, focus on your own progress and celebrate your own achievements, no matter how small they may seem.

The practice of gratitude is another powerful tool for cultivating self-love. By regularly acknowledging and appreciating the positive aspects of your life and yourself, you can shift your focus away from what you lack and towards what you have. This can improve your overall outlook and increase your sense of self-worth. Keeping a gratitude journal, where you write down things you are thankful for each day, can be a simple yet effective way to incorporate gratitude into your daily routine.

Forgiveness is a vital aspect of self-love. Holding onto past mistakes or harboring resentment towards yourself can be incredibly damaging. Self-forgiveness involves letting go of past transgressions and understanding that everyone makes mistakes. It means learning from your experiences and moving forward with a renewed sense of purpose and self-compassion. By forgiving yourself, you allow yourself to heal and grow.

Self-love is also about embracing your uniqueness. Each person has a distinct set of qualities, talents, and experiences that make them who they are. Embracing your individuality means celebrating what makes you different and recognizing that these differences are strengths, not weaknesses. By appreciating your uniqueness, you can build a stronger sense of identity and self-worth.

The journey to self-love is not always easy, and it often requires ongoing effort and practice. It is a dynamic process that evolves over time as you grow and change. There will be setbacks and challenges along the way, but each step forward is a step towards a healthier and more fulfilling relationship with yourself.

One practical way to cultivate self-love is through the use of daily affirmations. Affirmations are positive statements that can help you overcome negative thoughts and self-doubt. By regularly repeating affirmations, you can reprogram your mind to focus on your strengths and potential. For example, saying to yourself, "I am worthy of love and respect," or "I am capable of achieving my goals," can reinforce a positive self-image and boost your confidence.

Another effective practice is mindfulness. Mindfulness involves paying attention to the present moment without judgment. It can help you become more aware of your thoughts and feelings and allow you to respond to them with compassion rather than criticism. Mindfulness can be practiced through meditation, deep breathing exercises, or simply by taking a few moments each day to focus on your surroundings and your inner experiences. By incorporating mindfulness into your daily routine, you can develop a greater sense of calm and self-acceptance.

The Role of Daily Affirmations

Daily affirmations serve as powerful tools in the journey toward self-love and personal growth. They help reshape your mindset, bolster self-esteem, and foster a positive outlook on life. By regularly engaging in the practice of affirmations, you can begin to counteract negative thoughts and beliefs that have taken root over time and replace them with empowering, supportive statements.

Affirmations are positive statements that you repeat to yourself, often out loud, to influence your subconscious mind. They work by planting seeds of positive thought, which can grow into a more optimistic and confident self-perception. The key is consistency; daily repetition helps solidify these new, positive beliefs.

Imagine waking up each morning and the first thing you do is look into the mirror and say, "I am worthy of love and respect." Such a simple statement, yet it carries immense power. Over time, as you continue to affirm this belief, it begins to sink in, altering the way you perceive yourself and interact with the world.

The psychological impact of affirmations is backed by research in cognitive psychology. Studies have shown that the brain has a remarkable ability to adapt and change, a concept known as neuroplasticity. By consistently exposing your brain to positive affirmations, you can create new neural pathways that support a healthier, more positive self-image. This process can help reduce stress, improve resilience, and enhance overall well-being.

Crafting effective affirmations requires mindfulness and intention. The most impactful affirmations are those that resonate deeply with you and address specific areas where you seek growth or change. They should be positive, present-tense statements that reflect your desired reality. For instance, instead of saying, "I will be confident," say, "I am confident." This phrasing helps your mind accept the affirmation as a current truth rather than a future possibility.

Incorporating affirmations into your daily routine can be both simple and transformative. Start your day with a few minutes dedicated to repeating your affirmations. This practice sets a positive tone for the day and helps ground you in your intentions. You might choose to write them down, say them out loud, or even meditate on them. The method matters less than the consistency and sincerity with which you practice.

Throughout the day, find moments to reinforce your affirmations. For example, during a break at work, take a few deep breaths and repeat an affirmation silently to yourself. This can help recenter your thoughts and maintain a positive mindset amidst daily challenges. Evening reflections can also be a powerful time to engage in affirmations. As you wind down, reaffirm your positive beliefs and acknowledge your progress. This practice can help you end the day on a positive note and promote restful sleep.

One common challenge in maintaining a daily affirmation practice is overcoming initial skepticism or discomfort. It is normal to feel awkward or doubt the effectiveness of affirmations at first. However, it is crucial to persist. Like any new habit, it takes time and patience to see results. Trust the process and remind yourself that change does not happen overnight.

Personalizing your affirmations can make them more meaningful and effective. Tailor them to address your unique experiences, goals, and desires. If you struggle with self-esteem, affirmations like "I am enough just as I am" or "I deserve happiness and success" can be particularly powerful. If you are working towards a specific goal, such as a career change or personal project, affirmations like "I am capable and confident in my abilities" can help reinforce your commitment and belief in yourself.

Real-life stories of individuals who have transformed their lives through daily affirmations abound. Take, for example, the story of Sarah, a young woman who struggled with self-doubt and anxiety. She began incorporating daily affirmations into her morning routine, focusing on statements like "I am strong and capable" and "I trust myself to handle whatever comes my way." Over time, Sarah noticed a significant shift in her mindset. She felt more confident, resilient, and empowered to take on new challenges. Her relationships improved, and she found greater satisfaction in her work and personal life.

Another powerful example is John, a middle-aged man facing a difficult career transition. By using affirmations such as "I am open to new opportunities" and "I am worthy of success," John was able to navigate the uncertainty with a positive outlook. These affirmations helped him stay motivated and focused, ultimately leading to a successful career change that brought him greater fulfillment and satisfaction.

Challenges will inevitably arise as you integrate affirmations into your life. Doubt, impatience, and external negativity can all undermine your efforts.

However, maintaining a consistent practice and reminding yourself of the benefits can help you stay committed. It can also be helpful to track your progress. Keep a journal where you note any changes in your thoughts, feelings, and behaviors as you continue your affirmation practice. This can provide tangible evidence of your growth and reinforce your commitment.

To further support your affirmation practice, consider pairing it with other self-care activities. Physical exercise, healthy eating, mindfulness meditation, and adequate sleep can all enhance the effectiveness of your affirm ations by creating a supportive environment for positive change. For instance, combining a morning workout with affirmations can boost your energy and set a positive tone for the day. Mindfulness meditation before bed, paired with affirmations, can help you unwind and solidify your positive beliefs before sleep.

How to Use This Book Effectively

Embarking on a journey of self-improvement and personal growth can be both exciting and daunting. This book is designed to be your companion, guide, and source of inspiration as you navigate this path. To make the most of the insights and practical advice contained within, it's essential to approach the material with an open mind, a willingness to engage actively, and a commitment to integrating what you learn into your daily life.

First, set aside dedicated time for reading and reflection. Personal growth isn't something that happens passively; it requires intentional effort and focus. Consider establishing a routine where you spend a specific amount of time each day or each week with this book. This could be in the morning when your mind is fresh, during a lunch break to reinvigorate your day, or in the evening as a way to wind down and reflect. Consistency in your reading habits will help reinforce the concepts and practices discussed, making it easier to integrate them into your life.

As you read, engage actively with the material. Take notes on key points that resonate with you, highlight passages that you find particularly insightful, and jot down any questions or reflections that arise. This active engagement will help deepen your understanding and retention of the material. Don't be afraid to pause and reflect on what you've read before moving on to the next section. Sometimes, taking a moment to digest and contemplate a concept can lead to greater clarity and insight.

In addition to active reading, consider discussing the material with others. Sharing your thoughts and reflections with friends, family, or a support group can provide new perspectives and enhance your understanding. These discussions can also offer valuable opportunities for feedback and accountability, which can be crucial for maintaining motivation and progress in your personal growth journey.

Applying the practical advice and exercises provided in this book is essential for real change. Theory alone is not enough; you must put what you learn into practice. Start by choosing one or two exercises or techniques that resonate with you and commit to incorporating them into your daily routine. For example, if the book suggests a daily gratitude practice, set aside a few minutes each day to write down things you are grateful for. As you become comfortable with these initial practices, gradually introduce additional exercises and techniques. This gradual integration allows you to build sustainable habits without becoming overwhelmed.

Tracking your progress is another key component of using this book effectively. Consider keeping a journal where you document your experiences, reflections, and any changes you notice over time. This can serve as both a record of your journey and a source of motivation when you encounter challenges. Reviewing your journal periodically can also help you identify patterns and insights that may not be immediately apparent.

Flexibility and adaptability are important as you work through the book. Personal growth is not a linear process; it involves ups and downs, detours, and moments of breakthrough. Be patient with yourself and open to adjusting your approach as needed. If a particular exercise or technique isn't resonating with you, don't be afraid to modify it or try something different. The goal is to find what works best for you and supports your unique journey.

It's also beneficial to revisit chapters or sections that are particularly relevant to you at different points in your journey. As you grow and evolve, your needs and challenges may change. What resonated with you initially might take on new meaning or offer different insights when revisited later. This book is a resource that you can return to again and again, drawing new wisdom and guidance from its pages as you continue to develop.

Maintaining a growth mindset is crucial throughout this process. Embrace the idea that personal growth is a lifelong journey, and there is always room for learning and improvement. Challenges and setbacks are inevitable, but they are also opportunities for growth and learning. Approach each obstacle with curiosity and a willingness to learn, rather than frustration or self-criticism.

Self-compassion is another essential element. Personal growth can sometimes bring up difficult emotions or highlight areas where we feel we are falling short. It's important to treat yourself with kindness and understanding during these moments. Recognize that everyone has strengths and weaknesses, and that growth involves both celebrating your progress and acknowledging areas for improvement without judgment.

Creating a supportive environment can significantly enhance your ability to use this book effectively. Surround yourself with people who encourage and support your growth. This might include friends, family members, mentors, or a community group focused on personal development. Sharing your goals and progress with supportive individuals can provide motivation and accountability, making it easier to stay committed to your journey.

Balance is key. While it's important to dedicate time and effort to personal growth, it's also crucial to maintain balance in your life. Make sure to prioritize self-care, rest, and relaxation alongside your growth efforts. Overextending yourself can lead to burnout and diminish the effectiveness of your efforts. Strive for a balanced approach that allows for sustainable, long-term growth.

Consider incorporating complementary resources and activities into your personal growth journey. This might include books, podcasts, workshops, or classes that align with your interests and goals. Engaging with a variety of resources can provide new perspectives and insights, enriching your overall experience.

In addition to external resources, embrace the use of internal resources such as mindfulness and introspection. Regularly practicing mindfulness can help you stay present and aware of your thoughts, feelings, and behaviors. This heightened awareness can make it easier to notice when you're falling into old patterns and to consciously choose new, more supportive actions. Introspection, on the other hand, allows you to delve deeper into your motivations and desires, providing clarity and direction for your personal growth efforts.

Setting Your Intentions for the Journey

Embarking on any journey requires a clear sense of direction, and personal growth is no exception. Setting your intentions is the first crucial step in this transformative process. Intentions serve as the guiding principles that shape your actions, decisions, and mindset. They are more than mere goals; they are the underlying motivations that fuel your journey and give it purpose. By setting clear and meaningful intentions, you can navigate the path of personal growth with greater clarity and determination.

Begin by taking a moment to reflect on why you are embarking on this journey. What aspects of your life do you wish to change or improve? This initial reflection is essential as it provides the foundation upon which your intentions will be built. Consider all areas of your life, including your relationships, career, health, and personal fulfillment. Identifying the areas that need attention will help you establish focused and relevant intentions.

Next, think about the values that are most important to you. Values are the core beliefs that guide your behavior and decision-making. They are deeply personal and unique to each individual. For some, values might include honesty, compassion, and growth, while for others, they might be creativity, resilience, and balance. By aligning your intentions with your core values, you ensure that your journey is authentic and meaningful.

Once you have identified your values, translate them into specific intentions. For example, if one of your core values is growth, your intention might be to continually seek new learning opportunities and challenge yourself to step out of your comfort zone. If compassion is a key value, your intention might be to practice kindness and empathy in all your interactions. The more specific and actionable your intentions are, the more powerful they will be in guiding your journey.

Writing down your intentions can significantly enhance their impact. There is something inherently powerful about putting pen to paper; it solidifies your commitment and makes your intentions tangible. Consider keeping a dedicated journal for this purpose. Write your intentions clearly and revisit them regularly. This practice not only reinforces your commitment but also allows you to track your progress and make adjustments as needed.

It's also important to frame your intentions positively. Instead of focusing on what you want to avoid or eliminate, focus on what you want to cultivate and embrace. For instance, rather than setting an intention to "stop procrastinating," reframe it as "embrace proactive and timely action in all tasks." Positive framing helps to create a more constructive and motivating mindset.

As you set your intentions, be mindful of the language you use. Use affirming and empowering words that resonate with you. Phrases like "I am," "I choose," and "I commit" can be particularly effective. For example, instead of saying "I want to be more confident," state "I am confident in my abilities and decisions." This shift in language reinforces a sense of ownership and belief in your intentions.

Setting intentions is not a one-time event; it is an ongoing process. Life is dynamic, and as you grow and change, your intentions may need to evolve as well. Regularly revisit and revise your intentions to ensure they remain aligned with your current values and aspirations. This flexibility allows you to stay responsive to new insights and experiences, keeping your journey relevant and meaningful.

Incorporating visualization into your intention-setting process can further enhance its effectiveness. Visualization involves creating a mental image of yourself achieving your intentions. It is a powerful tool that can help you internalize your goals and increase your motivation. Take a few moments each day to visualize yourself living in alignment with your intentions. See yourself embodying the qualities and behaviors you aspire to cultivate. This practice can help to reinforce your commitment and make your intentions feel more attainable.

Sharing your intentions with a trusted friend, mentor, or support group can provide additional support and accountability. When others are aware of your intentions, they can offer encouragement, feedback, and guidance. They can also help to hold you accountable, ensuring that you stay committed to your journey even when challenges arise. Choose individuals who are supportive and invested in your growth, and be open to their insights and feedback.

In addition to sharing your intentions with others, consider creating a visual representation of your intentions. This could take the form of a vision board, a mind map, or even a simple list displayed in a prominent place. Visual reminders serve as constant reinforcements of your intentions, keeping them at the forefront of your mind. They can also provide a source of inspiration and motivation, especially during moments of doubt or difficulty.

As you move forward on your journey, it is important to remain patient and compassionate with yourself. Personal growth is a gradual process, and there will inevitably be setbacks and challenges along the way. Recognize that these obstacles are a natural part of the journey and do not reflect a failure on your part. Instead, view them as opportunities for learning and growth. Practice self-compassion and remind yourself that progress, no matter how small, is still progress.

Finally, celebrate your successes, both big and small. Acknowledging and celebrating your achievements reinforces your commitment to your intentions and provides a sense of accomplishment. Take time to reflect on how far you've come and the progress you've made. Celebrations don't have to be grandiose; they can be simple acts of self-care or moments of gratitude. By recognizing your achievements, you build positive reinforcement, making it more likely that you will continue to pursue your intentions with enthusiasm and dedication.

Overview of the Path Ahead

Setting out on a journey of personal growth can feel both exhilarating and daunting. To navigate this path effectively, it's crucial to have a clear understanding of what lies ahead. This overview will provide a roadmap, highlighting the key stages, potential challenges, and essential tools you'll need along the way.

Every journey begins with self-awareness. This initial stage involves a deep dive into understanding yourself—your strengths, weaknesses, values, and motivations. Self-awareness is the cornerstone of personal growth, as it provides the clarity needed to set meaningful goals. Reflect on your experiences, seek feedback from trusted sources, and consider engaging in practices such as journaling or meditation to enhance your self-awareness. This stage is about laying a solid foundation, so take your time to thoroughly explore and understand who you are.

With a firm grasp on self-awareness, the next step is setting goals. Goals give direction and focus to your journey. They should be specific, measurable, achievable, relevant, and time-bound (SMART). However, goal-setting is not just about ticking boxes; it's about aligning your goals with your deeper values and aspirations. This alignment ensures that your efforts are meaningful and fulfilling. Start with broad, long-term goals and then break them down into smaller, manageable steps. This approach makes the process less overwhelming and more achievable.

Once your goals are set, it's time to develop a plan. A well-thought-out plan acts as a roadmap, guiding you towards your goals. It involves identifying the resources, skills, and support systems you'll need. This might include further education, seeking mentorship, or building new habits. A good plan also anticipates potential obstacles and outlines strategies to overcome them. Be flexible and willing to adjust your plan as needed, recognizing that the journey of personal growth is often nonlinear and requires adaptability.

Execution is where the rubber meets the road. This stage is about taking consistent action towards your goals. It's easy to feel motivated at the beginning, but maintaining that momentum requires discipline and resilience. Establish routines that support your goals, and break tasks into smaller, more manageable chunks to avoid feeling overwhelmed. Celebrate small victories along the way to stay motivated. Remember, progress is often incremental and requires patience and perseverance.

As you move forward, you will inevitably encounter challenges. These can range from external obstacles such as lack of resources or time constraints to internal barriers like self-doubt and fear of failure. It's important to approach these challenges with a growth mindset—viewing them as opportunities for learning rather than setbacks. Develop problem-solving skills and resilience to navigate these hurdles. Surrounding yourself with a supportive community can also provide encouragement and perspective during tough times.

Reflection is a critical component of the journey. Regularly take time to assess your progress and reflect on your experiences. What has worked well? What hasn't? Reflection allows you to learn from your experiences and make necessary adjustments to your plan. It also helps you stay aligned with your values and goals, ensuring that your efforts remain meaningful. Consider keeping a journal to document your reflections and track your progress over time.

Adaptability is another key element of personal growth. Life is unpredictable, and circumstances can change suddenly. Being adaptable means being open to new information and willing to adjust your goals and plans as needed. This flexibility can prevent you from feeling stuck or discouraged when things don't go as planned. Embrace change as a natural part of the journey and look for ways to turn unexpected challenges into opportunities for growth.

Throughout this journey, it's important to cultivate a positive mindset. Your attitude can significantly impact your ability to achieve your goals. Practice gratitude, focus on your strengths, and maintain a hopeful outlook even in the face of adversity. Positive thinking doesn't mean ignoring challenges; rather, it means approaching them with a sense of possibility and confidence in your ability to overcome them.

Another crucial aspect of the path ahead is building a strong support system. Personal growth is not a solitary endeavor. Surround yourself with people who support and encourage your aspirations. This might include friends, family, mentors, or professional coaches. A supportive network can provide valuable feedback, motivation, and accountability. Don't hesitate to seek help or advice when needed, and be willing to offer support to others on their journeys as well.

As you advance, you will also need to focus on continuous learning. Personal growth is an ongoing process that requires a commitment to lifelong learning. Stay curious and open to new ideas, skills, and perspectives. Engage in activities that challenge you intellectually and creatively. This could involve reading, taking courses, attending workshops, or exploring new hobbies. Continuous learning keeps your mind active and adaptable, enriching your journey and expanding your horizons.

It's also important to maintain a healthy balance. Personal growth should enhance your overall well-being, not detract from it. Ensure that your efforts to grow and improve don't lead to burnout or neglect of other important areas of your life, such as relationships, health, or leisure. Strive for a balanced approach that allows you to pursue your goals while also enjoying a fulfilling and well-rounded life.

Finally, remember that the journey of personal growth is deeply personal and unique to each individual. Avoid comparing your progress to others. Everyone's path is different, and what works for one person may not work for another. Focus on your own journey and trust in your process. Celebrate your unique strengths and achievements, and use them as motivation to keep moving forward.

Chapter 2

The Foundation of Self-Love

Defining Self-Love: What It Is and What It Isn't

Self-love is a concept that is often misunderstood and misrepresented. Many people confuse it with selfishness or narcissism, but true self-love is far from either of these extremes. At its core, self-love is about recognizing your worth, treating yourself with kindness, and caring for your well-being. It's a foundational aspect of mental and emotional health, influencing how you interact with others and how you navigate life's challenges.

Defining self-love begins with understanding that it is a multifaceted practice. It encompasses self-respect, self-care, self-compassion, and self-acceptance. Self-respect involves knowing your worth and setting boundaries to protect your well-being. It means standing up for yourself and not allowing others to treat you poorly. Self-care is about taking deliberate actions to maintain your physical, mental, and emotional health. This includes everything from eating nutritious foods and exercising to taking time for rest and relaxation. Self-compassion involves being gentle with yourself, especially in times of failure or difficulty. It's about treating yourself with the same kindness and understanding that you would offer to a friend. Lastly, self-acceptance is about embracing all parts of yourself, including your flaws and imperfections. It's recognizing that you are inherently valuable, regardless of your achievements or mistakes.

What self-love isn't, is equally important to understand. It is not self-indulgence or selfishness. While self-love involves taking care of your needs, it doesn't mean putting your desires above those of others to their detriment. It's about finding a balance where you can prioritize your well-being without harming or neglecting the needs of others. Self-love is also not narcissism. Narcissism involves an inflated sense of self-importance and a lack of empathy for others, whereas self-love includes a healthy sense of self-worth and compassion both for yourself and others. Additionally, self-love is not about achieving perfection. It's about appreciating yourself as you are and striving for growth and improvement, not because you are flawed, but because you deserve to thrive.

To illustrate what self-love looks like in practice, consider the story of Sarah, a woman who spent years neglecting her own needs while trying to please everyone around her. She often felt exhausted, unappreciated, and resentful. One day, after a particularly draining week, Sarah realized that she needed to make a change. She started small, setting aside time each day for activities she enjoyed, like reading and going for walks. She also began to set boundaries, saying no to requests that would overextend her. Over time, Sarah noticed a significant improvement in her mood and energy levels. She felt more balanced and capable of offering genuine support to others without feeling depleted. Sarah's journey highlights that self-love is a gradual process of making choices that honor and respect your well-being.

To cultivate self-love, begin by practicing self-awareness. Pay attention to your thoughts, feelings, and behaviors. Notice how you speak to yourself—are you kind and encouraging, or critical and harsh? Start challenging negative self-talk and replacing it with affirmations and positive statements. For example, if you catch yourself thinking, "I'm not good enough," counter it with a statement like, "I am worthy and capable." This shift in mindset can gradually transform your inner dialogue into one that supports and uplifts you.

Another essential practice is setting boundaries. Boundaries are vital for protecting your time, energy, and emotional health. They help you maintain a sense of balance and prevent burnout. Setting boundaries might involve saying no to commitments that don't align with your priorities, limiting interactions with people who drain your energy, or carving out time for self-care activities. Remember that setting boundaries is not about shutting others out but creating a healthy space where you can thrive.

Engaging in regular self-care activities is also crucial for nurturing self-love. Self-care looks different for everyone, so it's important to find what works best for you. It might include physical activities, such as yoga or hiking, creative pursuits like painting or writing, or relaxation techniques like meditation or deep breathing exercises. The key is to make self-care a non-negotiable part of your routine. By regularly investing time in activities that rejuvenate and nourish you, you reinforce the message that you are worth caring for.

Practicing self-compassion is another powerful way to cultivate self-love. Life is full of ups and downs, and it's essential to be kind to yourself during challenging times. Instead of criticizing yourself for mistakes or shortcomings, try to view them as opportunities for growth and learning. When you experience failure or hardship, treat yourself with the same empathy and understanding you would offer a friend. Remind yourself that it's okay to be imperfect and that you deserve love and kindness, especially when things are tough.

Embracing self-acceptance is a fundamental aspect of self-love. This means acknowledging and appreciating all parts of yourself, including your strengths and areas for improvement. It's about letting go of the need for external validation and recognizing that your worth is inherent. Practicing self-acceptance involves embracing your unique qualities, quirks, and even the traits you may consider flaws. It's understanding that these aspects make you who you are and contribute to your individuality. Start by identifying parts of yourself that you struggle to accept and practice affirmations to reinforce a positive self-view. For instance, if you are critical of your appearance, remind yourself daily that beauty comes in many forms and that your worth isn't tied to your looks.

The Science behind Self-Love

The pursuit of self-love is not just a trendy concept; it's deeply rooted in science. Understanding the scientific basis for self-love can illuminate why it's so essential for our well-being and provide practical strategies for cultivating it. Self-love impacts our mental health, physical health, and overall quality of life, and research across psychology, neuroscience, and even biology supports this.

Psychology studies have long demonstrated the profound effects of self-love on mental health. Self-love, often measured through constructs like self-esteem and self-compassion, correlates strongly with lower levels of anxiety and depression. When individuals practice self-compassion, they tend to engage in healthier coping mechanisms during stressful times. Instead of resorting to self-criticism or avoidance, they are more likely to face challenges head-on with a balanced perspective. This resilience stems from the ability to treat oneself kindly, recognizing that mistakes and failures are part of the human experience.

The work of psychologist Kristin Neff, a pioneer in the field of self-compassion, offers valuable insights. Neff defines self-compassion as treating oneself with the same kindness and understanding that one would offer to a friend. Her research indicates that people who practice self-compassion experience greater psychological well-being, including increased happiness, life satisfaction, and emotional intelligence. Self-compassion also buffers against the negative effects of perfectionism and fear of failure, allowing individuals to take risks and pursue personal growth without being paralyzed by the possibility of making mistakes.

Neuroscience provides further evidence of the benefits of self-love. Brain imaging studies reveal that self-compassion activates the brain's caregiving system, involving regions like the insula and the anterior cingulate cortex. These areas are associated with emotional regulation and empathy, suggesting that self-compassionate individuals are better equipped to manage their emotions and respond to stress. On the other hand, self-criticism activates the brain's threat-defense system, including the amygdala, which can lead to heightened stress responses and increased release of cortisol, the stress hormone. Chronic activation of this system is linked to various health issues, such as anxiety, depression, and cardiovascular problems.

Incorporating self-love into daily life can also have tangible physical health benefits. Studies have shown that individuals with higher levels of self-compassion have lower levels of inflammation, which is a key factor in many chronic diseases. This connection may be partly due to reduced stress levels, as chronic stress is known to exacerbate inflammation. Furthermore, self-love practices like mindfulness and meditation have been shown to improve immune function, suggesting that nurturing a positive relationship with oneself can bolster the body's defenses against illness.

The biological underpinnings of self-love extend to our genetic makeup as well. Research in the field of epigenetics explores how our behaviors and environment can influence gene expression. Positive psychological states, including self-love, can lead to beneficial changes in gene expression related to stress and immune function. For instance, a study published in the journal *Psychoneuroendocrinology* found that mindfulness meditation, a practice closely linked to self-love, can alter gene expression in ways that improve immune response and reduce inflammation. These findings suggest that self-love not only enhances mental and emotional well-being but also has a profound impact on our physical health at a molecular level.

Understanding the science behind self-love also involves recognizing the role of social connections. Human beings are inherently social creatures, and our relationships with others significantly influence our self-perception and mental health. Research indicates that individuals who experience supportive and validating relationships are more likely to develop a healthy sense of self-love. Conversely, those who endure critical or abusive relationships may struggle with self-criticism and low self-esteem. This underscores the importance of cultivating positive social environments and seeking out relationships that reinforce our worth and value.

A practical approach to fostering self-love involves integrating scientifically-backed strategies into daily routines. Mindfulness is one such strategy, with a substantial body of research supporting its benefits. Mindfulness involves paying attention to the present moment with an attitude of non-judgment and acceptance. Practicing mindfulness can help individuals become more aware of their thoughts and feelings, making it easier to recognize and counteract self-critical tendencies. Techniques such as mindful breathing, body scans, and meditation can be effective tools for cultivating self-compassion and reducing stress.

Another powerful strategy is cognitive restructuring, a technique from cognitive-behavioral therapy (CBT). This involves identifying and challenging negative thought patterns and replacing them with more balanced and realistic ones. For example, if someone consistently thinks, "I'm not good enough," cognitive restructuring would encourage them to examine the evidence for and against this belief and develop a more compassionate and accurate self-view. This process can significantly reduce self-criticism and enhance self-love over time.

Physical self-care is also crucial in the pursuit of self-love. Engaging in regular physical activity, eating a balanced diet, and ensuring adequate sleep are foundational practices that support overall well-being. Exercise, in particular, has been shown to boost mood and reduce symptoms of anxiety and depression, partly due to the release of endorphins, the body's natural mood elevators. Additionally, physical activity can improve self-esteem and body image, further reinforcing a positive sense of self.

Common Myths and Misconceptions

Often, the path to understanding a topic is clouded by myths and misconceptions that can distort our perception and hinder progress. In the realm of self-care and personal development, these false beliefs can be particularly pervasive, leading many astray in their quest for improvement. By debunking these myths, we can pave the way for a clearer, more effective approach to enhancing our well-being.

One prevalent myth is that self-care is synonymous with self-indulgence. Many people equate self-care with activities like luxurious spa days, expensive vacations, or splurging on non-essential items. While these activities can be enjoyable and sometimes beneficial, true self-care is far broader and more nuanced. It encompasses a wide range of practices aimed at maintaining and improving one's physical, mental, and emotional health. Simple, everyday actions like getting enough sleep, eating nutritious foods, exercising regularly, and setting boundaries are foundational aspects of self-care that have profound impacts on overall well-being. Viewing self-care as mere indulgence can trivialize its importance and deter individuals from integrating essential self-care practices into their daily lives.

Another common misconception is that self-care is selfish. This belief stems from the idea that prioritizing one's own needs inherently means neglecting the needs of others. In reality, effective self-care enables individuals to better care for those around them. When we take the time to replenish our own energy and resources, we are more capable of supporting others. Think of the oxygen mask principle on airplanes: you're instructed to put on your own mask before assisting others. This is because you can't help anyone if you're incapacitated. Similarly, neglecting self-care can lead to burnout, stress, and decreased effectiveness, ultimately diminishing our ability to contribute positively to the lives of others.

A related myth is the notion that self-care is a luxury that only those with ample free time and resources can afford. This misconception overlooks the fact that self-care is essential for everyone, regardless of their circumstances. While it's true that some forms of self-care might require financial investment or time, many effective self-care practices are accessible and low-cost or even free. Activities such as mindfulness meditation, deep breathing exercises, walking in nature, and journaling can all be incorporated into daily routines without significant expense. Additionally, prioritizing self-care doesn't necessarily mean carving out large chunks of time; even small, consistent actions can have a meaningful impact.

The idea that self-care is a one-size-fits-all solution is another myth that can be misleading. There is no universal approach to self-care that works for everyone. Each person's needs, preferences, and circumstances are unique, which means self-care should be personalized. What works well for one individual might not be effective for another. For example, some people might find solace in social activities and spending time with friends, while others might need solitude and quiet to recharge. Understanding and honoring these differences is crucial for developing a self-care routine that is truly beneficial. It's important to experiment with various practices and pay attention to what genuinely makes you feel better.

Another widespread misconception is that self-care is only necessary when you're feeling stressed or overwhelmed. While it's true that self-care can help manage stress, it's not solely a reactive measure. Proactive self-care—practicing habits that support well-being on a regular basis—can prevent stress and burnout from occurring in the first place. By integrating self-care into your daily routine, you build resilience and create a buffer against life's inevitable challenges. This proactive approach helps maintain a steady state of well-being rather than constantly playing catch-up when things become difficult.

The belief that self-care is merely a trend is another misconception that can undermine its significance. While it's true that self-care has gained popularity in recent years, it is far from a passing fad. The principles of self-care are rooted in longstanding traditions and practices across various cultures and disciplines, including psychology, medicine, and philosophy. The contemporary emphasis on self-care reflects a growing recognition of its importance in our fast-paced, high-stress world. Dismissing self-care as a trend risks ignoring the substantial body of evidence supporting its benefits and the enduring need for practices that promote holistic health.

A particularly harmful myth is the idea that seeking help for mental health issues is a sign of weakness. This stigma can prevent individuals from accessing the support and care they need. In reality, recognizing when you need help and taking steps to get it is a sign of strength and self-awareness. Mental health is an integral part of overall well-being, and seeking professional help, whether through therapy, counseling, or other support services, is a vital aspect of self-care. Addressing mental health issues proactively can lead to significant improvements in quality of life and should be encouraged rather than stigmatized.

The misconception that self-care requires eliminating all stress from one's life is another fallacy that can set unrealistic expectations. Some level of stress is inevitable and even necessary for growth and development. The goal of self-care is not to eliminate stress entirely but to manage it effectively and prevent it from becoming overwhelming. Healthy stress management involves recognizing stressors, developing coping strategies, and maintaining a balance between challenges and relaxation. Techniques such as time management, mindfulness, and setting realistic goals can help mitigate the negative effects of stress. Understanding that stress is a natural part of life allows for a more balanced and sustainable approach to self-care.

The Benefits of Embracing Self-Love

The journey toward self-love might appear daunting, but the rewards of embracing this practice are profound and far-reaching. When we cultivate self-love, we unlock a multitude of benefits that enhance our mental, emotional, and physical well-being, enriching our lives in ways we may not initially realize.

One of the most significant benefits of embracing self-love is the improvement in mental health. Self-love fosters a positive self-image and helps combat negative self-talk, which is often at the root of many mental health challenges. When we practice self-love, we begin to challenge and reframe the critical inner voices that undermine our confidence and self-worth. This shift can lead to a reduction in symptoms of anxiety and depression, as we replace self-criticism with self-compassion. By treating ourselves with kindness and understanding, we create a more supportive internal environment that promotes mental resilience.

Embracing self-love also enhances emotional well-being. When we love ourselves, we become more attuned to our emotions and better equipped to manage them. Self-love encourages us to acknowledge and validate our feelings rather than suppress or ignore them. This emotional awareness allows us to respond to life's challenges with greater equanimity and grace. We learn to set healthy boundaries, recognize our needs, and prioritize our well-being, which in turn fosters emotional stability and a deeper sense of inner peace.

Physical health is another area where the benefits of self-love are evident. When we value ourselves, we are more likely to engage in behaviors that support our physical well-being. This might include maintaining a balanced diet, exercising regularly, getting adequate sleep, and avoiding harmful habits such as smoking or excessive drinking. Self-love motivates us to care for our bodies not out of obligation, but out of a genuine desire to nurture and protect our well-being. This holistic approach to health can lead to improved energy levels, better immune function, and a lower risk of chronic diseases.

Relationships also thrive when we embrace self-love. When we have a healthy relationship with ourselves, we are better able to form and maintain positive relationships with others. Self-love enables us to communicate more effectively, set and respect boundaries, and engage in relationships that are mutually supportive and respectful. It also helps us recognize and walk away from toxic relationships that do not serve our well-being. By fostering self-love, we cultivate a sense of self-worth that empowers us to seek out and sustain healthy, fulfilling connections with others.

Self-love also boosts our resilience and ability to cope with adversity. Life is inherently unpredictable, and challenges are inevitable. However, when we love and believe in ourselves, we are better equipped to face these challenges head-on. Self-love provides a stable foundation from which we can draw strength and confidence, enabling us to navigate difficult situations with greater ease and less self-doubt. This resilience not only helps us overcome obstacles but also supports personal growth and development as we learn and evolve through our experiences.

Another profound benefit of self-love is the enhancement of self-awareness and personal growth.

Self-love encourages us to engage in introspection and self-reflection, helping us understand our values, desires, and aspirations more clearly. This self-awareness is crucial for personal development, as it allows us to identify areas where we want to grow and improve. By embracing self-love, we foster a mindset of continuous learning and self-improvement, which can lead to a more fulfilling and purpose-driven life.

Moreover, self-love can significantly impact our professional lives. When we value and believe in ourselves, we are more likely to pursue opportunities that align with our passions and strengths. Self-love boosts our confidence, helping us take risks and step out of our comfort zones in our careers. It also enables us to handle professional setbacks with grace and persistence, viewing them as opportunities for growth rather than reflections of our worth. This positive mindset can lead to greater job satisfaction, career advancement, and overall professional success.

Creativity and innovation are also nurtured by self-love. When we embrace and accept ourselves, we feel more comfortable expressing our unique perspectives and ideas. Self-love reduces the fear of judgment and failure, which often stifles creativity. By fostering a supportive internal environment, self-love encourages us to explore our creative potential and take bold, innovative steps in our personal and professional lives. This creative freedom can lead to new discoveries, solutions, and artistic expressions that enrich our lives and the lives of others.

In addition to these individual benefits, embracing self-love can have a positive ripple effect on our communities and society as a whole. When we love and care for ourselves, we model these behaviors for others, contributing to a culture of compassion and empathy. Self-love can inspire others to embark on their own journeys of self-discovery and self-care, creating a more supportive and understanding community. Furthermore, individuals who practice self-love are often more engaged and proactive in addressing social issues, as they recognize the interconnectedness of personal and collective well-being.

Finally, self-love enhances our overall quality of life. When we value and care for ourselves, we experience greater happiness, fulfillment, and contentment. Self-love allows us to appreciate our achievements, celebrate our strengths, and accept our imperfections. This balanced perspective fosters a sense of inner peace and joy that permeates all aspects of our lives. When we embrace self-love, we are more likely to pursue activities and experiences that bring us genuine happiness and satisfaction, rather than seeking external validation or approval.

Real-Life Transformations through Self-Love

Samantha had always struggled with self-esteem. Growing up, she constantly sought validation from others, believing her worth was tied to their approval. This pattern continued into adulthood, affecting her relationships, career, and overall happiness. It wasn't until she hit a particularly low point, overwhelmed by stress and self-doubt, that she decided something had to change. Samantha embarked on a journey of self-love, a decision that would transform her life in ways she never imagined.

At the outset, Samantha's daily routine included a simple yet profound practice: each morning, she stood in front of the mirror and said three positive things about herself. Initially, this felt awkward and insincere. However, persistence paid off. Over time, these affirmations began to reshape her self-perception. She started to believe in her own worth and capabilities, setting the stage for deeper changes.

Samantha's newfound self-love had a cascading effect on her career. Previously, she had hesitated to take on challenging projects, fearing failure and criticism. With her growing confidence, she began to embrace opportunities with enthusiasm. She took a bold step and proposed a new initiative at work, something she had been contemplating for months. Her idea was not only accepted but also praised for its creativity and potential impact. This success further boosted her confidence, leading to a series of professional achievements that eventually resulted in a promotion.

Relationships were another area where Samantha experienced significant transformation. She had always put others' needs before her own, often to her detriment. Learning to love herself meant recognizing the importance of setting boundaries and prioritizing her well-being. She started to communicate her needs more clearly and assertively. This shift in dynamics brought unexpected benefits. Her relationships became more balanced and fulfilling, as friends and family respected her newfound assertiveness. She also distanced herself from toxic relationships that drained her energy and self-esteem, making room for more supportive and positive connections.

Samantha's story is one of many that illustrate the profound impact of self-love. Consider John, a middle-aged man who had always been his own harshest critic. John's self-esteem issues stemmed from a childhood filled with constant comparisons to his more academically successful siblings. This deep-seated insecurity followed him into adulthood, affecting his career choices and personal life. John decided to seek therapy, where he learned about the importance of self-compassion and self-acceptance.

Through therapy, John began to challenge the negative beliefs he held about himself. He learned to celebrate his strengths and achievements, rather than focusing on perceived shortcomings. This shift in mindset led to a remarkable transformation. John, who had always played it safe in his career, decided to pursue his passion for writing. He started a blog where he shared his experiences and insights, which quickly gained a following. Encouraged by this success, he wrote a book that became a bestseller. John's journey from self-doubt to self-acceptance not only changed his life but also inspired countless others through his writing.

The power of self-love is not limited to adults. Children and teenagers can also experience life-changing transformations when they learn to value themselves. Emma, a high school student, struggled with body image issues and bullying. Her self-esteem plummeted, affecting her academic performance and social life. Emma's parents decided to enroll her in a self-esteem workshop designed for teens. There, Emma learned about the importance of self-acceptance and the dangers of comparing herself to others.

With the support of her family and the tools she gained from the workshop, Emma began to see herself in a new light. She started journaling about her feelings and practicing gratitude, focusing on her strengths and achievements. This newfound self-love empowered Emma to stand up to her bullies and seek out friends who valued and respected her. Her academic performance improved, and she became more engaged in extracurricular activities. Emma's transformation was a testament to the resilience and strength that self-love can foster in young people.

In addition to these personal stories, research supports the transformative power of self-love. Studies have shown that individuals who practice self-compassion experience lower levels of anxiety and depression and higher levels of life satisfaction. Self-love promotes a positive self-image, which is crucial for mental and emotional well-being. It also enhances resilience, enabling individuals to cope more effectively with stress and adversity.

One study conducted by Dr. Kristin Neff, a leading researcher in self-compassion, found that people who practice self-compassion are more likely to engage in healthy behaviors, such as exercising regularly, eating well, and getting enough sleep. These behaviors contribute to overall physical health and well-being. Furthermore, self-love has been linked to better relationship satisfaction. When individuals value and respect themselves, they are more likely to attract and maintain healthy, fulfilling relationships.

The practice of self-love can take many forms, and its impact can be seen in various aspects of life. For instance, consider the story of Carlos, an entrepreneur who struggled with imposter syndrome. Despite his success, Carlos constantly doubted his abilities and feared being exposed as a fraud. This anxiety affected his business decisions and overall well -being. Determined to overcome these feelings, Carlos started working with a coach who specialized in self-compassion and mindfulness.

Chapter 3

Understanding Affirmations

What Are Affirmations?

Affirmations are powerful tools for personal development, rooted in the concept that our thoughts and words shape our reality. They are positive statements that individuals repeat to themselves to counteract negative self-talk and reinforce positive beliefs. The practice of using affirmations can be traced back to ancient civilizations, but it gained widespread popularity in the modern world through the work of self-help pioneers like Louise Hay and Norman Vincent Peale.

Imagine waking up each morning feeling overwhelmed by the challenges of the day ahead. This was the reality for Jessica, a busy mother of two who juggled a demanding job and household responsibilities. The constant stress took a toll on her mental and physical health. One day, a friend introduced her to the concept of affirmations. Skeptical but desperate for change, Jessica decided to give it a try. She started with simple affirmations like, "I am capable of handling whatever comes my way," and "I am worthy of love and respect."

Initially, Jessica felt awkward and self-conscious repeating these statements. However, she persisted, incorporating them into her daily routine. She would recite her affirmations in front of the mirror each morning and again before bed. Over time, Jessica noticed a shift in her mindset. The affirmations helped her reframe her thoughts, replacing self-doubt with confidence and positivity. She felt more resilient and better equipped to manage her responsibilities. Jessica's story is a testament to the transformative power of affirmations.

Affirmations work by influencing the subconscious mind, which governs our habitual thoughts and behaviors. When we repeatedly affirm positive statements, we begin to internalize these beliefs, leading to changes in our attitudes and actions. This process is supported by research in psychology and neuroscience. Studies have shown that positive affirmations can reduce stress, increase self-esteem, and improve overall well-being.

For example, a study published in the journal "Social Cognitive and Affective Neuroscience" found that self-affirmation activates the brain's reward centers, promoting feelings of well-being and reducing the impact of stress. Another study from Carnegie Mellon University demonstrated that participants who practiced self-affirmation before a stressful task showed lower levels of the stress hormone cortisol and performed better than those who did not use affirmations.

To harness the power of affirmations, it is essential to understand how to create effective ones. Effective affirmations are positive, present-tense statements that reflect what you want to achieve or believe. They should be specific, realistic, and emotionally resonant. For instance, instead of saying, "I will not be anxious," you might say, "I am calm and in control." The former focuses on the negative state you want to avoid, while the latter emphasizes the positive state you want to achieve.

Consider the story of Mark, a young entrepreneur facing the daunting task of launching his own business. Mark struggled with self-doubt and fear of failure, which hindered his progress. With the guidance of a mentor, Mark developed a set of affirmations tailored to his goals and challenges. He started each day with affirmations like, "I am a successful and confident entrepreneur," and "I attract opportunities and resources that help my business thrive."

By consistently repeating these affirmations, Mark gradually shifted his mindset. He became more confident in his abilities and more proactive in seeking out opportunities. His business began to grow, and he attributed much of his success to the positive impact of affirmations on his mindset and behavior.

Affirmations can be incorporated into various aspects of daily life. One effective method is to pair affirmations with visualization. Visualization involves creating a mental image of yourself achieving your goals or embodying the qualities you desire. This technique enhances the power of affirmations by engaging both the conscious and subconscious mind.

For example, Sarah, a professional athlete, used affirmations and visualization to prepare for a major competition. Each day, she would repeat affirmations like, "I am strong, focused, and ready to win," while visualizing herself crossing the finish line and celebrating her victory. This practice helped Sarah build confidence and maintain a positive mindset, contributing to her success in the competition.

Another practical way to use affirmations is to integrate them into your environment. Write your affirmations on sticky notes and place them where you will see them frequently, such as on your bathroom mirror, computer screen, or refrigerator. This constant exposure reinforces the positive messages and helps to embed them in your subconscious mind.

Affirmations can also be woven into your daily routine through activities like journaling or meditation. When journaling, dedicate a section to writing down your affirmations and reflecting on how they make you feel. This practice can deepen your connection to the affirmations and enhance their effectiveness. During meditation, repeat your affirmations silently or aloud, focusing on the meaning and emotional resonance of each statement.

It's important to remember that affirmations are not a quick fix; they require consistency and patience. The benefits of affirmations accumulate over time as the positive messages reshape your beliefs and behaviors. It's also crucial to approach affirmations with an open mind and a willingness to embrace change. Skepticism can undermine the effectiveness of affirmations, so it's essential to give this practice a genuine effort and trust in the process.

The Psychological Impact of Affirmations

The psychological impact of affirmations is profound, touching on various aspects of human cognition and emotion. To understand this impact, consider the story of Daniel, a high school teacher who had always struggled with imposter syndrome. Despite his qualifications and years of experience, he constantly felt inadequate and feared being exposed as a fraud. His negative self-talk was relentless, often leading to anxiety and self-doubt. One day, a colleague suggested he try using affirmations to counter these feelings.

Daniel was skeptical but decided to give it a shot. He started with simple affirmations like, "I am a knowledgeable and capable teacher," and "I am confident in my abilities." He repeated these statements daily, especially before entering his classroom. Over time, Daniel noticed a shift in his mindset. The affirmations began to override his negative thoughts, allowing him to feel more confident and grounded in his role. His teaching improved, and he felt a renewed sense of purpose and satisfaction in his work.

This transformation can be explained by understanding how affirmations work on a psychological level. Affirmations are designed to reprogram the subconscious mind, replacing negative beliefs with positive ones. The practice is grounded in the principles of cognitive-behavioral therapy (CBT), which posits that our thoughts influence our emotions and behaviors. By changing our internal dialogue through affirmations, we can alter our emotional responses and actions.

Research supports the effectiveness of affirmations in promoting psychological well-being. A study conducted by researchers at Carnegie Mellon University found that self-affirmation exercises can buffer stress and improve problem-solving abilities. Participants who engaged in self-affirmation before a stressful task were more likely to stay calm and perform better than those who did not.

Furthermore, affirmations have been shown to enhance self-esteem and self-worth. Low self-esteem is often rooted in negative self-perceptions and critical self-talk. Affirmations help to counteract these negative patterns by reinforcing positive beliefs about oneself. For instance, repeating affirmations like, "I am worthy of love and respect," can gradually erode the deep-seated beliefs that contribute to low self-esteem.

Consider the case of Maria, a young woman who struggled with body image issues. Growing up, she was constantly bombarded with negative messages about her appearance from peers and media. This led to a cycle of self-criticism and low self-worth. When Maria discovered affirmations, she decided to focus on statements that celebrated her body and its strengths. She repeated affirmations like, "I love and accept my body as it is," and "I am strong and capable." Over time, these affirmations helped Maria develop a healthier relationship with her body, boosting her self-esteem and overall well-being.

Affirmations also play a crucial role in fostering a growth mindset, a concept popularized by psychologist Carol Deck. A growth mindset is the belief that abilities and intelligence can be developed through effort and perseverance. Affirmations that emphasize growth and learning, such as "I embrace challenges and learn from them," can help individuals cultivate this mindset. This shift in perspective can lead to greater resilience, motivation, and a willingness to take on new challenges.

For example, consider the experience of David, an aspiring musician. David often felt discouraged by setbacks and failures, questioning his talent and potential. By incorporating affirmations like, "I grow and improve with each practice session," and "Every challenge is an opportunity to learn," he began to view obstacles as part of the learning process. This change in mindset not only improved his skills but also reignited his passion for music.

The psychological impact of affirmations extends beyond individual benefits; it can also enhance relationships and social interactions. Negative self-beliefs can hinder our ability to connect with others, leading to feelings of isolation and loneliness. Affirmations that focus on social confidence and self-acceptance can improve our interactions and relationships. For instance, affirmations like, "I am open to forming meaningful connections," and "I am worthy of healthy and supportive relationships," can help individuals approach social situations with greater confidence and openness.

Consider the story of John, who had always felt socially awkward and anxious in group settings. His fear of judgment and rejection often led him to avoid social events, exacerbating his loneliness. When John started using affirmations that emphasized his social worth and confidence, he gradually became more comfortable in social situations. He noticed that as his self-confidence grew, so did his ability to connect with others. This not only improved his social life but also enhanced his overall happiness and mental health.

On a broader scale, affirmations can contribute to a more positive and compassionate society. When individuals practice affirmations, they are likely to become more empathetic and supportive towards others. Positive self-talk fosters a sense of inner peace and contentment, which can translate into more harmonious interactions with those around us. This ripple effect can create a more positive environment, whether in families, workplaces, or communities.

To maximize the psychological benefits of affirmations, it is important to practice them consistently and mindfully. This means setting aside dedicated time each day to repeat your affirmations, preferably in a quiet and focused setting. Consistency helps to reinforce the positive messages, making them more likely to be internalized and reflected in your thoughts and behavior.

How Affirmations Influence Self-Perception

Jordan had always been his harshest critic. Every time he looked in the mirror, he saw flaws. Despite being successful in his career as a software developer, he constantly doubted his abilities and felt unworthy of his achievements. His self-perception was marred by years of internalized negativity, a common struggle for many. Then, on a friend's advice, Jordan started practicing affirmations. He began with simple statements: "I am capable," "I am deserving of success," and "I am proud of my achievements." Slowly, these affirmations began to chip away at his negative self-image, revealing a more confident, self-assured individual.

The way affirmations influence self-perception is rooted in their ability to rewire our thought patterns. Self-perception, or the way we see and think about ourselves, is profoundly influenced by the narratives we continuously tell ourselves. These narratives can either be empowering or debilitating. Affirmations act as a tool to consciously shape these narratives in a positive direction.

One of the primary mechanisms through which affirmations influence self-perception is by counteracting negative self-talk. Negative self-talk can be insidious, often operating below the level of conscious awareness. It reinforces limiting beliefs and self-doubt. Affirmations, on the other hand, introduce positive, empowering statements that can gradually replace these negative thoughts. This shift doesn't happen overnight; it's a process of consistent repetition and reinforcement.

Consider the example of Emily, a college student who struggled with severe anxiety during exams. Her internal dialogue was filled with fears of failure and inadequacy. After learning about affirmations, she began using statements like, "I am prepared and capable," and "I trust in my ability to succeed." Repeating these affirmations daily, especially before exams, helped Emily change her self-perception from one of anxiety and doubt to one of confidence and calm. Her academic performance improved as a result, illustrating the power of positive self-perception.

The psychological principle behind this transformation is known as cognitive restructuring, a key component of cognitive-behavioral therapy (CBT). Cognitive restructuring involves identifying and challenging negative thought patterns and replacing them with more balanced and positive ones. Affirmations are a practical tool for this process, providing a structured way to introduce and reinforce positive thoughts.

Scientific research supports the effectiveness of affirmations in improving self-perception and overall mental health. A study published in the journal *Social Cognitive and Affective Neuroscience* found that self-affirmation activates the brain's reward centers, enhancing feelings of self-worth and reducing stress. This neural evidence underscores the potential of affirmations to foster a more positive self-view.

Moreover, affirmations can help expand one's self-concept, which is the collection of beliefs about oneself. A narrow self-concept can limit one's potential by focusing on perceived weaknesses and failures. Affirmations encourage a broader, more inclusive self-concept that acknowledges strengths, achievements, and potential. For instance, if someone believes they are not good at public speaking, they might use affirmations like, "I am a confident and effective communicator." Over time, this can help them see themselves in a new light, capable of mastering public speaking.

Take the story of Raj, a mid-level manager who avoided speaking at meetings due to his fear of public speaking. He started using affirmations such as, "I communicate clearly and confidently," and "My voice matters." With consistent practice, Raj's self-perception began to shift. He no longer saw himself as someone who shied away from speaking but as a confident communicator. This new self-perception empowered him to actively participate in meetings, significantly enhancing his professional presence and opportunities for advancement.

In addition to reshaping how we see ourselves, affirmations can also influence how we believe others perceive us. This phenomenon, known as the "looking-glass self," suggests that our self-perception is partly shaped by how we think others view us. Positive affirmations can help us project confidence and self-assuredness, which in turn can influence others to see us in a positive light. This feedback loop further reinforces a positive self-perception.

For example, Lisa, a young entrepreneur, often felt intimidated when pitching her business ideas to potential investors. She feared being seen as inexperienced and unworthy of investment. By using affirmations like, "I am a talented and innovative entrepreneur," and "Investors see the value in my ideas," she started to project more confidence during her pitches. This change in self-perception influenced how investors saw her, leading to more positive responses and successful funding for her projects.

The practice of affirmations also aligns with the theory of self-fulfilling prophecies. This theory suggests that our beliefs and expectations can influence our behavior, which in turn can lead to the fulfillment of those beliefs. When we use affirmations, we are setting positive expectations for ourselves. These positive expectations can influence our actions, leading to outcomes that reinforce our new, more positive self-perception.

Moreover, affirmations can be particularly powerful when combined with visualization. Visualization involves imagining oneself achieving goals or embodying desired qualities. When paired with affirmations, visualization helps to create a vivid mental image of success and reinforces the positive statements we repeat to ourselves, making them more tangible and believable.

Crafting Effective Affirmations

Sarah woke up every morning dreading the day ahead. Her internal dialogue was a constant barrage of negativity: "I'm not good enough," "I'll never succeed," "Why would anyone care about what I have to say?" Her self-esteem was at an all-time low, and it showed in her work and personal life. On a particularly tough day, a friend introduced her to the concept of affirmations—positive statements that challenge negative thoughts. Skeptical but desperate for change, Sarah decided to give it a try. Little did she know, this simple practice would transform her life.

Crafting effective affirmations is an art that requires intention, clarity, and consistency. The first step is understanding what an affirmation is. An affirmation is a positive statement that reflects a desired reality. It is designed to replace negative self-talk with empowering thoughts. When crafted and used correctly, affirmations can reshape our mindset, boost our confidence, and improve our overall well-being.

The most effective affirmations are personal and specific. Generic statements like "I am happy" or "I am successful" may not resonate deeply enough to create change. Instead, affirmations should be tailored to address specific areas of one's life that need improvement. For instance, if someone struggles with self-worth, an affirmation like "I am worthy of love and respect" can be more impactful. Specificity helps the affirmation feel more relevant and believable, which strengthens its effectiveness.

Another crucial element in crafting effective affirmations is the use of positive language. Affirmations should focus on what you want to achieve or believe, rather than what you want to avoid. For example, instead of saying "I am not afraid of failure," a more effective affirmation would be "I embrace challenges and learn from them." This subtle shift in language emphasizes a positive outcome and reinforces a constructive mindset.

Affirmations should also be stated in the present tense. This helps to create a sense of immediacy and reality, making it easier for the mind to accept and internalize the statement. Saying "I will be confident" implies that confidence is a future goal, potentially creating a sense of distance. In contrast, "I am confident" asserts that confidence is a current state of being, which can be more empowering and effective.

Consistency is key when it comes to affirmations. Like any new habit, the benefits of affirmations accrue over time with regular practice. It is important to integrate affirmations into daily routines, making them a natural part of one's lifestyle. Repeating affirmations daily—ideally, multiple times a day—helps to reinforce the positive messages and gradually rewire negative thought patterns.

One effective technique for integrating affirmations into daily life is to pair them with existing routines. For instance, affirmations can be repeated during morning and evening rituals, such as while brushing your teeth or preparing for bed. This consistency ensures that affirmations become a regular part of your thought process. Additionally, writing affirmations in a journal or placing them on sticky notes around your home or workspace can serve as constant reminders to practice positive thinking.

Visualization can also enhance the power of affirmations. Visualization involves creating a mental image of achieving your goals or embodying desired qualities. When paired with affirmations, visualization helps to create a vivid and tangible sense of success. For example, if your affirmation is "I am a confident public speaker," you might visualize yourself giving a successful presentation, feeling calm and composed. This practice not only reinforces the affirmation but also conditions your mind to expect and work towards the desired outcome.

Belief in the affirmations is another critical factor. If you find it hard to believe in a particular affirmation, start with something more believable and gradually work your way up. For example, if "I am wealthy and successful" feels too far-fetched, you might start with "I am becoming more financially secure every day." As your confidence grows and your self-perception improves, you can adjust your affirmations to reflect higher aspirations.

Measuring the impact of affirmations is also important to ensure they are effective. Regularly reflecting on your progress can help you determine whether your affirmations are working or if they need to be adjusted. Keep a journal to track changes in your thoughts, feelings, and behaviors. Note any improvements in your confidence, mood, or performance. This practice not only helps to monitor your progress but also reinforces the positive changes, providing additional motivation to continue.

Affirmations can also be crafted to address different aspects of life, including personal growth, relationships, career, and health. For personal growth, affirmations might focus on self-acceptance, resilience, or learning. For example, "I am constantly growing and evolving" or "I am resilient and overcome challenges with ease." In relationships, affirmations can emphasize qualities like compassion, understanding, and love, such as "I am a loving and supportive partner" or "I attract positive and healthy relationships."

In a professional context, affirmations can help to build confidence, motivation, and success. Statements like "I am a valuable and skilled employee" or "I achieve my goals with determination" can bolster self-belief and drive. For health and well-being, affirmations might focus on strength, vitality, and self-care, such as "I am strong and energetic" or "I prioritize my health and well-being."

Examples of Powerful Affirmations

In the dim light of dawn, Alex sat at his kitchen table with a cup of coffee and a notebook. He had read about the transformative power of affirmations and decided to give them a try. At first, the words felt foreign, almost silly, but he was determined to change the negative self-talk that had plagued him for years. Little did he know, these affirmations would soon become the cornerstone of his personal growth.

Crafting powerful affirmations requires a blend of introspection and precision. The most effective affirmations are those that resonate deeply with the individual and target specific areas of improvement or aspiration. Here are some examples that illustrate the various ways affirmations can be tailored to different aspects of life:

For self-confidence, consider affirmations that reinforce your worth and capabilities. Statements like "I am worthy of all the good things that happen to me" or "I have the power to create change in my life" can be particularly potent. These affirmations work by challenging the internal narratives that undermine self-esteem. When repeated consistently, they help to build a foundation of confidence and self-assurance.

In the realm of career and success, affirmations can motivate and inspire action. For instance, "I am a valuable asset to my team" or "I am capable of achieving my career goals" can instill a sense of purpose and direction. By focusing on your strengths and potential, these affirmations encourage a proactive approach to professional development, fostering a mindset geared towards growth and achievement.

Health and well-being affirmations are equally important, as they promote a positive relationship with your body and mind. Examples include "I am strong, healthy, and full of energy" or "I honor my body by making healthy choices." These statements not only encourage physical health but also support mental and emotional well-being. By affirming your commitment to self-care, you reinforce behaviors that contribute to a balanced and healthy lifestyle.

Relationships, whether familial, romantic, or platonic, can also benefit from targeted affirmations.

Statements like "I am surrounded by love and support" or "I communicate with honesty and compassion" can enhance your interactions with others. These affirmations help to cultivate a positive environment, fostering connections based on mutual respect and understanding.

For those seeking personal growth and self-improvement, affirmations that emphasize learning and resilience can be particularly effective. Consider affirmations such as "I am constantly learning and growing" or "I embrace challenges as opportunities for growth." These statements encourage a growth mindset, where obstacles are viewed as stepping stones rather than setbacks. By reinforcing your commitment to personal development, you pave the way for continuous improvement and self-discovery.

To illustrate the transformative power of affirmations, let's revisit Alex's journey. Each morning, he would write down affirmations that resonated with his goals and aspirations. "I am deserving of success" was one that stood out to him. At work, Alex had always felt overshadowed by his colleagues, doubting his skills and contributions. But as he repeated this affirmation daily, he began to notice subtle changes. He started volunteering for projects, sharing his ideas more freely, and gradually, his confidence grew. His manager took note of his increased engagement and initiative, leading to new opportunities and responsibilities.

In addition to writing and repeating affirmations, Alex incorporated visualization techniques. Each time he recited "I am a confident and effective leader," he would close his eyes and visualize himself leading a successful team meeting, his colleagues attentive and engaged. This mental imagery helped to bridge the gap between his current reality and his desired future, making his affirmations feel more attainable and real.

For many, the challenge lies in maintaining consistency and belief in the affirmations. It's important to remember that affirmations are not instantaneous solutions but tools for gradual change. They require patience and daily practice. One way to enhance their impact is by integrating them into a routine. Alex, for example, set reminders on his phone to recite his affirmations throughout the day—during his morning commute, lunch break, and before bed. This regular practice helped to ingrain the positive statements into his subconscious, slowly but surely reshaping his inner dialogue.

Affirmations can also be adapted to suit changing goals and circumstances. As Alex's confidence grew, he modified his affirmations to reflect his evolving aspirations. "I am a confident and effective leader" became "I lead my team to success with vision and empathy." This evolution ensured that his affirmations remained relevant and motivating, driving him to continually strive for higher levels of achievement and personal growth.

Moreover, combining affirmations with other positive practices can enhance their effectiveness. Alex found that pairing his affirmations with gratitude journaling amplified their impact. Each evening, he would write down three things he was grateful for, followed by his affirmations. This practice helped to cultivate a positive mindset, making it easier to believe in the affirmations and their potential to bring about change.

It's also beneficial to share your affirmations with a trusted friend or mentor. Alex confided in his friend, Sarah, who was also on a journey of self - improvement. They decided to support each other by sharing their affirmations and progress during their weekly catch-ups. This mutual accountability added another layer of commitment, making it harder to skip the practice. Sarah's encouragement and feedback provided Alex with additional insights and motivation, reinforcing the belief that change was indeed possible.

Chapter 4

Creating Your Personal Affirmation Practice

Setting Up a Daily Routine

The alarm buzzed at 6:00 AM, stirring Emma from her slumber. She stretched, feeling the familiar tug of resistance to leave the comfort of her bed. But today was different. Today marked the beginning of her new daily routine, a structured plan she had meticulously crafted to bring balance and productivity into her life. As she reached for her journal on the bedside table, Emma felt a surge of excitement and determination.

Emma's journey to establishing a daily routine began with understanding the importance of structure. Like many, she had struggled with the chaos of unplanned days, where tasks blended into one another, and productivity felt like a distant dream. The first step in her transformation was acknowledging that a well-structured routine could provide the framework needed to achieve her goals, manage her time effectively, and reduce stress.

Creating a daily routine starts with identifying priorities. Emma began by listing her daily responsibilities and long-term goals. She recognized that her work, health, personal development, and relationships were the pillars of her life. By categorizing her activities, she could allocate time slots to each, ensuring a balanced approach to her day.

Mornings set the tone for the entire day, so Emma decided to start with a morning routine that energized and prepared her for the tasks ahead. She began by waking up at the same time every day, even on weekends, to regulate her internal clock. This consistency helped her body adjust, making it easier to wake up and feel refreshed. Upon waking, she spent ten minutes practicing mindfulness meditation, focusing on her breath and setting positive intentions for the day. This practice helped clear her mind and reduce anxiety.

Next, Emma incorporated physical activity into her morning. She alternated between yoga and a brisk 30-minute walk, which not only boosted her physical health but also elevated her mood and mental clarity. Following her exercise, she dedicated time to a healthy breakfast, ensuring she fueled her body with nutritious foods that sustained her energy levels throughout the morning.

With her body and mind prepared, Emma moved on to her most critical work tasks. She adopted the "Eat That Frog" approach, tackling her most challenging and important tasks first. By addressing these tasks while her energy levels were highest, she found she could complete them more efficiently, leaving her with a sense of accomplishment that motivated her for the rest of the day.

Mid-morning, Emma scheduled a short break to stretch and hydrate. These mini-breaks were essential in preventing burnout and maintaining focus. She used this time to step away from her desk, take a few deep breaths, and reset her mind.

As noon approached, Emma transitioned into her lunchtime routine. She prepared a balanced meal, avoiding the temptation of quick, unhealthy options. During lunch, she stepped outside whenever possible, enjoying the fresh air and a change of scenery. This break was crucial in recharging her energy and maintaining a positive outlook for the afternoon.

Emma's post-lunch routine focused on less demanding tasks, such as emails, meetings, and administrative duties. She found that scheduling these activities during her natural energy dip allowed her to remain productive without requiring intense focus. To combat the afternoon slump, she incorporated a brief power nap or a quick walk, which revived her energy levels and prevented the lethargy that often accompanied this time of day.

As the workday concluded, Emma dedicated the late afternoon to personal development. She allocated time for reading, learning new skills, or working on passion projects. This period was a chance to invest in herself and her future, ensuring continuous growth and fulfillment.

Evenings were reserved for winding down and connecting with loved ones. Emma made it a point to disconnect from work and digital devices, creating a clear boundary between her professional and personal life. She enjoyed cooking dinner with her partner, engaging in meaningful conversations, and practicing gratitude for the day's experiences. This time helped strengthen her relationships and provided a sense of balance and contentment.

Before bed, Emma established a calming nighttime routine. She dimmed the lights, turned off electronic devices, and engaged in relaxing activities such as reading or journaling. Reflecting on her day, she noted her achievements and areas for improvement, setting goals for the next day. This practice not only helped her unwind but also provided a sense of closure and readiness for the following day.

Emma's journey to setting up a daily routine was not without challenges. Initially, she struggled with consistency and the temptation to revert to old habits. However, she reminded herself that forming new habits takes time and perseverance. By gradually introducing changes and forgiving herself for occasional slip-ups, Emma maintained her commitment to her routine.

One key to Emma's success was flexibility. While she adhered to a general structure, she allowed room for adjustments. Life is unpredictable, and rigid routines can lead to frustration when unexpected events arise. Emma learned to adapt her schedule, ensuring that her routine remained supportive rather than restrictive.

Additionally, Emma discovered the power of accountability. She shared her routine goals with a close friend, who also sought to establish a daily routine. They checked in with each other regularly, offering support and encouragement. This mutual accountability created a sense of camaraderie and motivation, making it easier to stay on track. Knowing that someone else was rooting for her success and facing similar challenges provided Emma with an extra layer of commitment.

Integrating Affirmations into Your Morning Ritual

The sun had just started to peek through the curtains when Laura's alarm went off at 6:30 AM. Unlike her previous groggy mornings, she felt a sense of purpose as her feet touched the floor. Today, she was beginning a new practice that she had heard could transform her mindset and set a positive tone for her entire day. She had decided to integrate affirmations into her morning ritual.

Laura had always been skeptical about affirmations, dismissing them as mere words without real impact. However, after reading several success stories and understanding the psychological benefits, she felt ready to give it a try. She knew that the morning was a critical time for setting intentions and shaping her mindset for the day ahead.

Her first step was to choose affirmations that resonated with her goals and values. Laura spent an evening crafting a list of positive statements that she genuinely believed in. She focused on areas where she wanted to see growth and change: self-confidence, productivity, and emotional well-being. Her list included affirmations such as, "I am capable of achieving my goals," "I am focused and productive," and "I approach each day with a positive mindset."

To make affirmations a seamless part of her morning, Laura paired them with existing habits. She placed her list of affirmations next to her bathroom mirror, ensuring she would see them first thing in the morning. As she brushed her teeth, she read each affirmation aloud, looking at herself in the mirror. This practice of speaking affirmations while making eye contact with her reflection helped to reinforce the messages and made them feel more personal and powerful.

Laura also decided to incorporate affirmations into her meditation practice. After her brief physical exercise routine—a mix of stretching and yoga—she sat quietly in a comfortable position, closed her eyes, and took a few deep breaths. Once she felt centered, she began to repeat her affirmations silently. This meditative state allowed her to internalize the positive messages deeply, setting a calm and focused tone for her day.

To enhance the impact of her affirmations, Laura used visualization techniques. As she repeated each affirmation, she visualized herself embodying the qualities and achieving the outcomes she desired. When she said, "I am confident in my abilities," she pictured herself successfully presenting in a meeting, receiving positive feedback from her colleagues. This imagery made the affirmations feel more real and attainable, bridging the gap between her current state and her desired future.

Consistency was key to making affirmations an effective part of Laura's morning ritual. She committed to practicing them daily, even on weekends. To keep herself accountable, she tracked her progress in a journal. Each morning after her affirmations, she spent a few minutes writing about how she felt and any noticeable changes in her mindset or behavior. This reflection helped her stay motivated and provided tangible evidence of her progress.

As weeks passed, Laura began to notice subtle but significant shifts in her mindset. She felt more confident tackling her daily tasks and approached challenges with a positive attitude. The affirmations seemed to be rewiring her brain, gradually replacing self-doubt and negativity with self-assurance and optimism. Her productivity improved as well; she found it easier to focus on her work and stay organized throughout the day.

Laura's morning affirmations also had a ripple effect on other areas of her life. She became more mindful of her self-talk throughout the day, catching and correcting negative thoughts before they could take root. This mindfulness extended to her interactions with others, making her more patient and compassionate. She noticed that her relationships with colleagues and loved ones improved as she approached them with a more positive and open mindset.

One particularly challenging morning, Laura woke up feeling anxious about a presentation she had to give later that day. Her first instinct was to let the anxiety take over, but she quickly turned to her affirmations. She stood in front of the mirror and repeated, "I am well-prepared and confident," "I communicate clearly

and effectively," and "I handle challenges with grace."
As she spoke these words, she felt her anxiety lessen.
The affirmations reminded her of her capabilities and
helped her approach the presentation with a calm and
focused mind. The presentation went smoothly, and
her confidence received a significant boost.

To keep her affirmations fresh and relevant, Laura
periodically updated her list. She added new
affirmations that reflected her evolving goals and
aspirations. For example, when she decided to
prioritize her health and fitness, she included
affirmations like, "I honor my body with healthy
choices," and "I am strong and resilient." This practice
ensured that her affirmations remained aligned with
her current intentions and kept her morning ritual
engaging and dynamic.

Laura's experience with integrating affirmations into
her morning ritual illustrates the transformative
power of this practice. It's not just the words
themselves, but the consistency, belief, and emotional
connection that make affirmations effective. By
starting her day with positive and empowering
statements, she set a tone of confidence and optimism
that carried through her day.

For those interested in adopting this practice, here are
some practical tips based on Laura's journey: Choose
affirmations that resonate deeply. Select statements
that reflect your personal goals, values, and areas
where you seek growth. Authenticity is crucial—
affirmations should feel true to your desires and
aspirations.

Using Affirmations throughout the Day

Samantha had always believed in the power of positive thinking, but it wasn't until she started using affirmations throughout her day that she truly experienced a transformation in her life. She had read about the benefits of affirmations—positive statements that can help reprogram your subconscious mind and encourage you to believe in certain things about yourself or your environment. However, she initially confined this practice to her morning routine. It was only when she extended the use of affirmations beyond the morning that she began to see profound changes.

One of the first adjustments Samantha made was incorporating affirmations into her workday. As a project manager, her days were often filled with back-to-back meetings, tight deadlines, and the constant need to juggle multiple tasks. This high-pressure environment frequently left her feeling overwhelmed and stressed. To counter this, she decided to integrate affirmations into her daily work routine.

Samantha started her workday by setting an intention. Before opening her laptop or diving into her email inbox, she took a moment to repeat an affirmation such as, "I am focused and efficient," or "I handle challenges with calm and clarity." She found that taking this brief pause helped her approach her tasks with a more centered and positive mindset.

Throughout the day, Samantha used affirmations as a tool to manage stress and maintain focus. Whenever she felt her stress levels rising or encountered a difficult situation, she took a few deep breaths and repeated a calming affirmation like, "I am in control of my emotions," or "I remain calm and composed under pressure." These moments of mindfulness not only reduced her stress but also improved her overall productivity and decision-making.

Samantha also discovered the power of using affirmations during breaks. She made it a point to step away from her desk for short breaks every couple of hours. During these breaks, she practiced stretching and took a few minutes to repeat positive affirmations. Statements like, "I am recharging and renewing my energy," and "I am grateful for this moment of rest," helped her feel more rejuvenated and ready to tackle the rest of her day.

One of the most significant changes Samantha noticed was in her interactions with colleagues. She started using affirmations to foster positive relationships and effective communication. Before meetings, she would repeat affirmations such as, "I communicate clearly and effectively," and "I listen with empathy and understanding." This practice helped her build stronger connections with her team and improved her ability to collaborate and lead.

Samantha didn't limit affirmations to her work environment. She found them equally beneficial in her personal life. For instance, during her commute, instead of letting her mind wander to negative or stressful thoughts, she repeated affirmations like, "I am safe and protected on my journey," and "I am looking forward to a productive and positive day."

This shift in focus made her commute more pleasant and set a positive tone for the rest of her day.

At home, Samantha used affirmations to enhance her personal well-being and relationships. She incorporated them into her evening routine to unwind and reflect on her day. Before going to bed, she repeated affirmations like, "I am proud of what I accomplished today," and "I am grateful for the experiences of today." This practice helped her cultivate a sense of gratitude and self-acknowledgment, promoting restful sleep and preparing her for the next day.

Samantha also saw the impact of affirmations on her physical health. She began using them during her workouts, repeating statements like, "I am strong and resilient," and "I enjoy taking care of my body." These affirmations motivated her to push through challenging exercises and maintain a positive attitude towards her fitness routine.

The key to Samantha's success with affirmations was consistency and personalization. She made affirmations a regular part of her day, ensuring they were always relevant to her current situation and goals. This dynamic approach kept her affirmations fresh and meaningful, allowing her to fully embrace their power.

For those interested in integrating affirmations throughout their day, here are some practical tips based on Samantha's experience:

1. **Begin with Intention**: Start your day with a clear intention. Choose an affirmation that

aligns with your goals for the day and repeat it before engaging in your daily tasks.

2. **Use Affirmations as Stress Relievers**: Whenever you feel stressed or overwhelmed, take a moment to breathe deeply and repeat a calming affirmation. This practice can help you regain control of your emotions and approach challenges with clarity.

3. **Incorporate Affirmations into Breaks**: Use your breaks as an opportunity to recharge both physically and mentally. Pair stretching or a short walk with positive affirmations to boost your energy and focus.

4. **Enhance Communication and Relationships**: Before meetings or interactions, repeat affirmations that promote effective communication and empathy. This can improve your relationships and collaboration with others.

5. **Transform Commutes**: Use travel time to repeat affirmations that promote safety, positivity, and anticipation for the day ahead. This can make your commute more enjoyable and set a positive tone for your activities.

6. **Integrate affirmations into your evening routine. Reflect on your achievements and experiences of the day with affirmations that foster gratitude and self-acknowledgment. This practice can promote relaxation and prepare you for restful sleep.

7. **Motivate Physical Activity**: During workouts or physical activities, use affirmations to encourage and motivate yourself. Statements that highlight your strength and resilience can help you push through challenging exercises and develop a positive attitude towards fitness.

8. **Stay Dynamic and Relevant**: Regularly update your affirmations to reflect your evolving goals and situations. Personalizing affirmations ensures they remain meaningful and impactful, keeping you engaged and motivated.

Evening Reflections and Affirmations

The quiet of the evening offered Lisa a moment of reprieve from the day's chaos. She had recently started a new practice that transformed her nights into a sanctuary of peace and introspection. Evening reflections and affirmations became her nightly ritual, a time to wind down and reconnect with herself. This practice brought her a sense of closure and calm that she had been missing for years.

Lisa began her journey with a simple decision: to set aside 15 minutes each night for herself. She needed a routine to help her transition from the busyness of the day to the tranquility of night. She found a comfortable spot in her bedroom, dimmed the lights, and lit a lavender-scented candle. This setup created an atmosphere conducive to relaxation and reflection.

Her evening reflections started with a gratitude practice. She kept a journal on her bedside table and wrote down three things she was grateful for each day. This exercise, though simple, had a profound effect on her outlook. By focusing on the positive aspects of her day, Lisa found herself going to bed with a sense of contentment. She realized that even on the toughest days, there were moments worth appreciating.

Next, Lisa incorporated a review of her day. She asked herself a series of questions: What went well today? What challenges did I face? How did I handle them? This reflective practice allowed her to acknowledge her achievements, no matter how small, and to think constructively about the challenges she encountered. Instead of letting mistakes or difficulties fester in her mind, she saw them as opportunities for growth. This shift in perspective was empowering and reduced her nightly anxiety.

After her reflections, Lisa turned to affirmations. She chose statements that resonated with her current goals and feelings. With the soft glow of the candle and the stillness of the night, she repeated affirmations like, "I am proud of what I accomplished today," "I am learning and growing every day," and "I release any stress or negativity from today." The act of speaking these affirmations aloud, in a calm and intentional manner, helped her internalize their messages.

To deepen the impact of her affirmations, Lisa combined them with visualization. She closed her eyes and envisioned herself embodying the qualities she affirmed. If she said, "I am confident and capable," she pictured herself successfully handling a challenging situation at work. This mental imagery made the affirmations more vivid and believable, reinforcing her positive self-talk.

Lisa also found that using affirmations before bed improved the quality of her sleep. By focusing on positive thoughts and releasing the day's stress, she created a mental environment conducive to rest. Her mind, no longer cluttered with worries and negative thoughts, could relax and drift into sleep more easily. Over time, she noticed a significant improvement in her sleep patterns and overall energy levels.

Another important aspect of Lisa's evening routine was setting intentions for the next day. After her reflections and affirmations, she spent a few minutes thinking about her goals and priorities for the following day. She wrote down one or two key intentions, such as "I will approach tomorrow with patience and positivity" or "I will focus on completing the project I started." This practice helped her wake up with a clear sense of purpose and direction.

Lisa's experience highlights the transformative power of evening reflections and affirmations. However, the key to her success lay in consistency. She committed to her nightly ritual, even on days when she felt tired or unmotivated. This dedication created a habit that became an integral part of her life, providing her with a reliable source of comfort and strength.

For those new to this practice, starting small can make the process more manageable. Begin with just a few minutes each night, gradually increasing the time as you become more comfortable. Choose affirmations that feel authentic and relevant to your current situation. Personalization is crucial—affirmations should resonate with your individual experiences and aspirations.

Incorporating evening reflections and affirmations into your routine can offer numerous benefits. It allows you to end your day on a positive note, fostering a sense of gratitude and accomplishment. Reflecting on your day helps you process your experiences constructively, reducing stress and promoting a growth mindset. Affirmations reinforce positive thinking and self-belief, preparing your mind for a restful sleep and a fresh start the next day.

One practical tip is to create a dedicated space for your evening ritual. This space should be comfortable and free from distractions, helping you associate it with relaxation and introspection. Using sensory elements like candles, soft lighting, or soothing music can enhance the ambiance and make the practice more enjoyable.

Another helpful approach is to vary your affirmations periodically. As your goals and circumstances change, update your affirmations to reflect these shifts. This keeps the practice dynamic and relevant, ensuring that it continues to resonate with you deeply.

For Lisa, her evening ritual became a cherished part of her day. It was a time to honor her experiences, celebrate her progress, and prepare for the future. The combination of reflections and affirmations provided her with a balanced approach to personal growth, blending self-awareness with positive reinforcement. This holistic practice not only improved her mental well-being but also had a ripple effect on other areas of her life, including her relationships, productivity, and overall happiness.

Overcoming Challenges in Maintaining Consistency

Maintaining consistency in any practice, whether it's a new habit, a workout regimen, or a professional goal, can be incredibly challenging. For Jane, a busy professional and mother of two, consistency seemed like an elusive dream. Despite her best intentions, she found it difficult to stick to her commitments. Her story is not unique. Many people struggle with maintaining consistency, facing a myriad of obstacles that can derail even the most well-laid plans. However, understanding these challenges and developing strategies to overcome them can make a significant difference.

One of the primary challenges Jane faced was time management. Balancing work, family, and personal time left her feeling stretched thin. She often felt there were simply not enough hours in the day to accomplish everything she set out to do. To tackle this, Jane began by identifying her priorities. She made a list of what was most important to her and what activities were non-negotiable. This helped her see where she could make adjustments and carve out dedicated time for her new habits.

Jane also realized the importance of setting realistic goals. Initially, she set ambitious targets that were difficult to achieve, leading to frustration and a sense of failure. By breaking down her goals into smaller, more manageable tasks, she found it easier to stay on track. For example, instead of committing to an hour of exercise every day, she started with 15 minutes and gradually increased the duration as she became more comfortable with the routine.

Another significant challenge Jane encountered was the lack of immediate results. In our fast-paced world, we often expect quick outcomes, and when they don't materialize, motivation can wane. Jane learned to shift her focus from immediate results to the process itself. She celebrated small milestones and progress, understanding that consistency would eventually lead to the larger results she desired. This mindset change helped her stay motivated even when progress seemed slow.

Accountability also played a crucial role in Jane's journey. She realized that sharing her goals with others and seeking support could help her stay committed. Jane joined a local fitness group and partnered with a friend who had similar goals. This sense of community provided encouragement and made her feel less alone in her struggles. Having someone to share her successes and setbacks with kept her motivated and accountable.

Distractions are another common hurdle in maintaining consistency. Jane found that her phone and social media were significant sources of distraction, often eating into the time she had set aside for her new habits. To combat this, she created a distraction-free environment during her dedicated habit time. She put her phone on silent, used apps that limited social media usage, and informed her family about her schedule so she wouldn't be disturbed.

Stress and fatigue also posed significant challenges. On particularly hectic days, Jane felt too exhausted to follow through with her commitments. Recognizing the importance of self-care, she incorporated relaxation techniques into her routine, such as deep breathing exercises and short meditation sessions. These practices helped her manage stress and maintain her energy levels, making it easier to stick to her habits.

Jane also discovered the power of habit stacking, a technique that involves linking a new habit to an existing one. For instance, she decided to do her daily reflections and affirmations right after brushing her teeth at night. By associating the new habit with an established one, she found it easier to remember and integrate it into her routine.

The fear of failure can be a significant barrier to consistency. Jane often felt discouraged by setbacks and was tempted to give up altogether. To overcome this, she adopted a growth mindset, viewing failures as opportunities for learning rather than as reflections of her abilities. She reminded herself that setbacks were a natural part of any journey and used them as motivation to improve and persevere.

Another technique that helped Jane maintain consistency was tracking her progress. She kept a journal where she logged her daily activities, noting what she accomplished and how she felt about it. This practice gave her a sense of achievement and allowed her to identify patterns and areas for improvement. By regularly reviewing her progress, she could make necessary adjustments and stay on course.

Jane also learned the importance of flexibility. Life is unpredictable, and rigid plans can often lead to frustration when things don't go as expected. She allowed herself some grace and adjusted her plans when necessary. If she missed a workout or skipped a reflection session, she didn't dwell on it. Instead, she focused on getting back on track the next day. This flexibility helped her maintain a positive attitude and avoid the all-or-nothing mentality that often derails consistency.

Finally, Jane realized that maintaining consistency required a strong sense of purpose. She took time to reflect on why her goals were important to her and how they aligned with her values. This deeper connection to her purpose provided the intrinsic motivation needed to stay committed, even when external rewards were not immediately visible.

Through these strategies, Jane overcame the challenges of maintaining consistency. Her journey was not without its ups and downs, but by understanding the obstacles and developing practical solutions, she was able to create lasting changes in her life. Her story serves as a testament to the fact that while maintaining consistency is challenging, it is also achievable with the right mindset and strategies.

Chapter 5

Affirmations for Building Self-Worth

Identifying Areas of Low Self-Worth

When it comes to personal growth and self-improvement, identifying areas of low self-worth is a crucial step. Low self-worth can manifest in various aspects of life, from career and relationships to personal health and well-being. Understanding where these feelings originate and how they affect behavior is essential for making meaningful changes. Take Sarah, for instance. A talented graphic designer, Sarah often struggled with feelings of inadequacy despite her evident skills. Her journey towards recognizing and addressing her low self-worth offers valuable insights.

Sarah's first clue came from her reluctance to take on new projects at work. Despite her manager's encouragement, she often doubted her abilities and feared failure. This hesitation wasn't due to a lack of skill; instead, it stemmed from a deep-seated belief that she wasn't good enough. Her self-doubt was a clear indication of low self-worth in her professional life. By acknowledging this, Sarah could begin to address the root cause rather than just the symptoms.

Another area where Sarah's low self-worth was evident was in her personal relationships. She frequently found herself in friendships and romantic relationships where she felt undervalued and taken for granted. Sarah often prioritized others' needs over her own, believing that her own desires were less important. This pattern of behavior not only affected her happiness but also reinforced her feelings of low self-worth. Recognizing this allowed Sarah to understand the importance of setting boundaries and valuing her own needs.

In social settings, Sarah often felt uncomfortable and out of place. She would stay on the fringes of conversations, afraid to share her thoughts and opinions. This social anxiety was another manifestation of her low self-worth. She worried that others would judge her harshly or find her uninteresting. By identifying this, Sarah realized that her worth wasn't dependent on others' approval and began working on building her confidence in social interactions.

Sarah's physical health also suffered due to her low self-worth. She neglected her well-being, often skipping meals or indulging in unhealthy foods. Exercise was sporadic, and she found it difficult to maintain a healthy routine. This neglect was a form of self-punishment, rooted in a belief that she didn't deserve to be healthy and happy. Understanding this connection was a pivotal moment for Sarah, prompting her to make more mindful choices about her health.

Financial habits can also reflect low self-worth. Sarah struggled with managing her finances, often overspending on items she didn't need as a way to compensate for her feelings of inadequacy. This behavior led to financial stress, which further exacerbated her low self-worth. By identifying this pattern, Sarah could address her spending habits and develop a healthier relationship with money.

One of the most profound areas where low self-worth manifested for Sarah was in her self-talk. She frequently engaged in negative self-talk, criticizing herself harshly for even minor mistakes. This internal dialogue was a constant reminder of her perceived inadequacies. Sarah's journey towards improving her self-worth began with changing this self-talk. She started practicing positive affirmations and reframing negative thoughts, which gradually shifted her mindset.

Sarah's experience highlights the importance of introspection in identifying areas of low self-worth. Journaling became a valuable tool for her, providing a safe space to explore her thoughts and feelings. Through regular journaling, she could track her progress, identify patterns, and celebrate small victories. This practice helped Sarah gain clarity and develop a deeper understanding of herself.

Seeking feedback from trusted friends and mentors also played a crucial role in Sarah's journey. She realized that her perception of herself was often skewed, and external perspectives could provide a more balanced view. Constructive feedback helped her recognize her strengths and areas for improvement, reinforcing her sense of self-worth.

Another effective strategy Sarah employed was setting SMART goals—Specific, Measurable, Achievable,

Relevant, and Time-bound. By breaking down her goals into manageable steps, she could track her progress and build confidence in her abilities. Achieving these small milestones provided a sense of accomplishment and reinforced her self-worth.

Sarah also found value in practicing gratitude. By focusing on the positive aspects of her life and acknowledging her achievements, she shifted her attention away from her perceived shortcomings. This practice helped her cultivate a more positive outlook and reinforced her sense of self-worth.

Therapy or counseling can be instrumental in addressing low self-worth. Sarah decided to seek professional help, which provided her with tools and strategies to understand and combat her negative beliefs. Therapy offered a safe space to explore her past experiences and how they shaped her self-perception. With the guidance of a therapist, Sarah could challenge her negative beliefs and develop healthier thought patterns.

In her journey, Sarah also discovered the importance of self-compassion. She learned to treat herself with the same kindness and understanding that she would offer a friend. This shift in perspective was crucial in building her self-worth. Instead of criticizing herself for her mistakes, she began to view them as opportunities for growth and learning.

Another key aspect of Sarah's journey was surrounding herself with positive influences. She sought out supportive friends and mentors who encouraged her and believed in her potential. These relationships provided a counterbalance to her negative self-perception and offered a network of support that was essential for her growth. Engaging with people who uplifted her helped Sarah slowly build a more positive and accurate image of herself.

Affirmations to Boost Self-Esteem

Affirmations are powerful tools that can significantly boost self-esteem when used effectively. They are positive statements that can help reprogram the subconscious mind, encouraging you to believe in your intrinsic worth and potential. Unlike fleeting moments of confidence, affirmations aim to create lasting change by altering the underlying beliefs that shape your self-image.

Consider the story of Mark, a young professional who struggled with self-doubt and low self-esteem. Despite being competent and hardworking, he often felt inadequate and unworthy of praise. He decided to give affirmations a try after reading about their potential benefits. Mark's journey with affirmations provides a compelling example of their transformative power.

Mark began his practice by identifying areas where he felt the most insecure. He realized that his self-doubt was most pronounced in social settings and at work. To address these issues, he crafted specific, positive affirmations. For his social anxiety, he used statements like, "I am confident and comfortable in social situations," and "I am worthy of respect and friendship." To combat his workplace insecurities, he repeated affirmations such as, "I am capable and skilled in my job," and "My contributions are valuable and appreciated."

The key to effective affirmations is repetition and belief. Mark incorporated his affirmations into his daily routine, repeating them each morning and evening. He also wrote them down and placed them in visible locations around his home and office. This constant exposure helped reinforce the positive messages, gradually replacing his negative self-talk with empowering beliefs.

Initially, Mark found it challenging to believe the affirmations he was reciting. This is a common hurdle for many people, as deeply ingrained negative beliefs can be resistant to change. However, persistence is crucial. Mark reminded himself that just as negative self-talk had taken years to develop, building positive self-esteem would also take time and consistent effort.

To enhance the effectiveness of his affirmations, Mark paired them with visualization techniques. He would close his eyes and imagine himself confidently engaging in social interactions or excelling at work. This mental imagery helped solidify the affirmations in his mind, making them feel more real and attainable. By visualizing his success, he could more easily bridge the gap between his current self-perception and the positive self-image he was striving to create.

Mark also discovered the importance of emotional engagement when practicing affirmations. Simply reciting words without feeling their truth can limit their impact. To fully engage with his affirmations, Mark focused on the emotions he wanted to experience, such as confidence, joy, and self-assurance. By tapping into these feelings, he made the affirmations more powerful and effective.

In addition to his personal practice, Mark sought support from friends and a mentor. He shared his affirmations with them and asked for their encouragement. This external validation helped reinforce his positive beliefs and provided additional motivation to continue his practice. Having a support system made the journey less isolating and more rewarding.

As weeks turned into months, Mark began to notice subtle but significant changes in his behavior and mindset. He felt more at ease in social settings, initiating conversations and expressing his thoughts without the usual fear of judgment. At work, he started taking on new challenges with increased confidence, and his contributions were recognized by his colleagues and superiors. The positive changes in his external circumstances mirrored the internal transformation he was experiencing.

Mark's story illustrates that affirmations can be a powerful tool for boosting self-esteem, but they require commitment and consistency. To maximize their effectiveness, it's important to create affirmations that are specific, positive, and phrased in the present tense. This helps the subconscious mind accept them as current realities rather than distant possibilities.

Another critical aspect of affirmations is their alignment with your core values and goals. Generic affirmations may have limited impact if they don't resonate with your personal aspirations. Take the time to reflect on what truly matters to you and craft affirmations that reflect those values. For example, if personal growth and learning are important to you, an affirmation like, "I am constantly growing and improving," may be particularly powerful.

Affirmations can also be integrated into other self-care practices to enhance their impact. For instance, combining them with mindfulness meditation can deepen your connection to the positive statements. During meditation, focus on your breath and repeat your affirmations silently, allowing them to sink deeply into your consciousness. This practice not only reinforces the affirmations but also helps cultivate a sense of inner peace and stability.

Journaling is another effective way to complement your affirmation practice. Each day, write down your affirmations and reflect on how they make you feel. Document any changes you notice in your thoughts, behaviors, and emotions. This process of self-reflection can provide valuable insights and help you track your progress over time.

It's also important to be patient with yourself throughout this journey. Building self-esteem through affirmations is not an overnight process. There may be days when you feel discouraged or doubt the effectiveness of your practice. During such times, remind yourself of the progress you've made and the long-term benefits of continuing your efforts. Each repetition of an affirmation is a step towards rewiring your mind and nurturing a healthier self-image.

Techniques for Reinforcing Positive Self-Image

Developing and maintaining a positive self-image can be transformative, influencing every aspect of one's life. It's about seeing yourself in a constructive and affirming light, which in turn nurtures confidence, resilience, and overall well-being. Various techniques can help reinforce a positive self-image, each serving as a step toward a healthier self-perception.

One powerful technique is practicing self-compassion. This involves treating yourself with the same kindness and understanding as you would offer to a good friend. When you make a mistake or face failure, instead of being overly critical, acknowledge your feelings, remind yourself that imperfection is part of the human experience, and offer words of comfort and support. Kristin Neff, a pioneering researcher in self-compassion, emphasizes that this practice can significantly enhance emotional resilience and reduce anxiety and depression.

Journaling is another effective method for reinforcing a positive self-image. By regularly writing about your thoughts and feelings, you can gain deeper insights into your inner world. Start by noting daily achievements, no matter how small. Reflect on positive feedback and accomplishments. Over time, this practice can shift your focus from self-criticism to self-appreciation, highlighting your strengths and progress. Additionally, journaling can help you track patterns and triggers of negative self-perception, allowing you to address and counteract them more effectively.

Visualization techniques can also play a crucial role in shaping a positive self-image. This involves creating vivid mental images of yourself succeeding and feeling confident. Athletes often use visualization to enhance performance, and it can be equally powerful for personal growth. Spend a few minutes each day visualizing scenarios where you excel in areas you typically struggle with. Imagine the sights, sounds, and emotions associated with your success. This mental rehearsal can help build a stronger, more positive self-image by making success feel more attainable and real.

Developing a growth mindset, a concept popularized by psychologist Carol Dweck, is essential for reinforcing a positive self-image. A growth mindset is the belief that abilities and intelligence can be developed through dedication and hard work. This perspective encourages you to view challenges as opportunities for learning rather than as threats to your self-worth. Embrace mistakes as valuable feedback and focus on the process of improvement instead of solely on outcomes. By cultivating a growth mindset, you can foster resilience and a more positive self-view, seeing yourself as capable of growth and change.

Another technique involves surrounding yourself with positive influences. The people we interact with can significantly impact our self-image. Seek out relationships that uplift and support you. Spend time with individuals who encourage your growth and celebrate your achievements. Conversely, limit exposure to those who consistently bring negativity or criticism into your life. Positive social interactions can reinforce your self-worth and help you build a more affirming self-image.

Affirmations, or positive self-statements, can also be a helpful tool. These are short, powerful phrases that you repeat to yourself to challenge and overcome negative thoughts. For affirmations to be effective, they need to be specific, positive, and in the present tense. For example, instead of saying, "I will try to be confident," say, "I am confident and capable." Repeat these affirmations daily, ideally in front of a mirror, to reinforce the positive beliefs about yourself. Over time, these statements can help shift your mindset and improve your self-image.

Mindfulness meditation can further support a positive self-image by helping you stay present and aware of your thoughts and feelings without judgment. Regular mindfulness practice can increase self-awareness and self-acceptance, reducing the impact of negative self-talk. By observing your thoughts from a distance, you can start to see them as transient and not necessarily true reflections of your worth. This detachment allows you to respond to negative thoughts with greater clarity and compassion, fostering a more positive self-image.

Engaging in activities that bring you joy and fulfillment can also strengthen your self-image. Whether it's a hobby, sport, or creative pursuit, doing something you love can provide a sense of accomplishment and boost your self-esteem. These activities allow you to express yourself authentically and experience moments of flow, where you are fully immersed and engaged. Such experiences can remind you of your capabilities and passions, reinforcing a positive view of yourself.

Another impactful technique is to set realistic and achievable goals. Break down larger aspirations into smaller, manageable steps. Celebrate each achievement, no matter how minor it might seem. This approach not only makes goals feel more attainable but also provides regular opportunities for success, boosting your confidence and reinforcing a positive self-image. Goal setting and accomplishment provide tangible evidence of your abilities and progress, countering negative self-perceptions.

Practicing gratitude can also shift your focus from what you lack to what you have. Keeping a gratitude journal, where you regularly write down things you are thankful for, can help cultivate a positive mindset. Over time, this practice can change your perspective, making you more aware of the positive aspects of yourself and your life. Gratitude helps you appreciate your strengths and achievements, which reinforces a positive self-image.

Finally, physical self-care is crucial in reinforcing a positive self-image. How you treat your body can significantly influence your perception of yourself. Regular exercise, a balanced diet, and sufficient rest are foundational to feeling good about yourself. Physical activity, in particular, releases endorphins, which can improve your mood and energy levels. Whether it's a morning jog, a yoga session, or a dance class, find activities that you enjoy and that make you feel strong and capable. Taking care of your physical health sends a powerful message to your subconscious that you are worth the effort and care, reinforcing a positive self-image.

Real-Life Stories of Enhanced Self-Worth

When Sarah first stepped into her new job at a bustling marketing firm, she felt a wave of excitement mixed with self-doubt. Fresh out of college, she wondered if she could meet the expectations of her experienced colleagues. Sarah's journey to enhanced self-worth began with small yet significant steps that gradually transformed her outlook on herself and her capabilities.

Sarah's initial strategy was to seek mentorship within the company. She approached Laura, a seasoned marketing manager known for her approachable demeanor. Laura's guidance was instrumental; she not only shared her professional knowledge but also offered Sarah a sense of validation and support that was crucial in those early days. Laura's belief in Sarah's potential helped her start to believe in herself. By setting manageable goals and celebrating each accomplishment, no matter how minor, Sarah began to build her confidence. This mentorship relationship highlighted the importance of having a supportive network in fostering self-worth.

Another story of transformation comes from James, a high school teacher who had always struggled with feelings of inadequacy. Despite his dedication to his students, he constantly felt that he wasn't doing enough. His turning point came when he decided to pursue further education, enrolling in a master's program in education. This decision was daunting, but James was determined to enhance his skills and, ultimately, his self-worth.

The journey through his master's program was not easy. Balancing teaching with studying demanded a lot from him, but James found that the more he learned, the more confident he became in his abilities. Notably, one of his courses emphasized reflective practice, encouraging him to regularly reflect on his teaching experiences and identify both strengths and areas for improvement. This reflective practice allowed James to see his growth and progress, which significantly boosted his self-worth. He began to realize that his efforts were making a real difference in his students' lives, something he had underestimated for years.

In a different setting, Maria's story unfolds in the healthcare arena. As a nurse, Maria was accustomed to long hours and high-stress situations. However, she often felt overshadowed by doctors and senior medical staff, which affected her self-esteem. Maria decided to take control of her narrative by specializing in pediatric care, an area she was passionate about. She enrolled in additional certification courses and participated in workshops that enhanced her expertise.

Maria's dedication paid off when she was able to implement new pediatric care protocols in her hospital. The positive feedback from her peers and the improved outcomes for her young patients were incredibly rewarding. These experiences solidified her belief in her professional capabilities. Moreover, Maria began to mentor new nurses, sharing her knowledge and experience, which further reinforced her sense of self-worth. Her story illustrates how setting and achieving professional goals can significantly enhance self-worth.

In the world of corporate finance, David's journey to enhanced self-worth began after a major career setback. He had been passed over for a promotion he felt he deserved, which led to a period of deep self-reflection. David realized that his self-worth had been too closely tied to external validation and career achievements. Determined to make a change, he started focusing on personal development and resilience.

David took up mindfulness meditation and joined a local community group that focused on personal growth. These activities helped him develop a more balanced view of himself, independent of his job title or salary. He also sought feedback from colleagues and mentors to understand his strengths better and areas where he could improve. Over time, David rebuilt his self-worth by recognizing his intrinsic value and not just his professional accomplishments. This shift in perspective not only improved his personal life but also led to better performance at work, eventually resulting in the promotion he had initially missed.

Emily's story is one of overcoming societal expectations. As a stay-at-home mom, she often felt undervalued and overlooked, both by society and herself. Emily loved her role but struggled with the perception that she wasn't contributing enough to her family or the world. Her journey to enhanced self-worth began when she decided to pursue her passion for writing.

Starting a blog about parenting and her personal experiences, Emily found a platform where she could express herself and connect with others. The positive feedback from readers and the supportive community she built online provided a sense of accomplishment and validation. Emily's blog grew into a successful venture, leading to speaking engagements and a book deal. Through this process, she realized that her worth was not defined by societal standards but by her unique contributions and passion. Emily's story underscores the importance of following one's passions and the profound impact it can have on self-worth.

In the artistic realm, consider the story of Alex, a painter who battled with self-doubt and criticism. For years, Alex compared his work to other artists, feeling that he fell short. His breakthrough came when he decided to focus on his unique style rather than trying to emulate others. Alex started to experiment with different techniques and mediums, finding joy in the creative process itself.

He began sharing his work at local art shows and online platforms, receiving positive feedback and constructive criticism. This external validation, coupled with his internal satisfaction from creating authentic art, significantly boosted his self-worth. Alex realized that his value as an artist lay in his individuality and the personal expression his work represented. Over time, Alex's confidence grew, and he even began teaching workshops, empowering other aspiring artists to find their voices. His journey highlights the importance of authenticity and self-expression in building self-worth.

Daily Exercises for Sustained Self-Worth

Every day presents an opportunity to build and sustain self-worth through consistent practices and exercises. These daily habits, when integrated into your routine, can significantly impact how you perceive yourself and your value. The following exercises are designed to be practical, actionable, and easy to incorporate into your daily life. By dedicating time each day to these activities, you can foster a deeper sense of self-worth that is resilient and enduring.

Start your day with a gratitude journal. Each morning, write down three things you are grateful for. This exercise shifts your focus from what you lack to what you have, fostering a sense of appreciation and positivity. Gratitude can improve your mood and outlook, setting a positive tone for the day ahead. Over time, regular practice of gratitude can help you recognize and value the good things in your life, thereby enhancing your self-worth.

Affirmations are another powerful tool. Craft a set of positive affirmations that resonate with you, such as "I am worthy of love and respect," or "I am capable and strong." Recite these affirmations aloud each morning. The repetition of positive statements can rewire your brain to believe in your inherent worth and potential. As you consistently affirm your value, you begin to internalize these beliefs, which can uplift your self-esteem and confidence.

Mindfulness meditation is an excellent practice to incorporate into your daily routine. Spend ten minutes each day in quiet reflection, focusing on your breath and observing your thoughts without judgment. Mindfulness helps you stay present and connected to yourself, reducing stress and anxiety. By cultivating a mindful state, you become more aware of your thoughts and feelings, allowing you to address negative self-talk and replace it with self-compassion. This practice fosters a deeper understanding and acceptance of yourself, which is crucial for sustained self-worth.

Physical exercise is not only beneficial for your body but also for your mind. Engage in at least 30 minutes of physical activity each day, whether it's walking, running, yoga, or strength training. Exercise releases endorphins, which are natural mood lifters. It also provides a sense of accomplishment and can improve your body image and self-perception. Regular physical activity reinforces the notion that you are taking care of your body, which in turn enhances your self-worth.

Set small, achievable goals each day. These goals can be related to your personal, professional, or emotional life. Completing these tasks gives you a sense of accomplishment and progress. It's important to acknowledge and celebrate these small wins, as they contribute to a positive self-image. By consistently achieving your daily goals, you reinforce the belief that you are capable and competent, which boosts your self-worth.

Journaling is a reflective practice that can significantly impact your self-worth. Spend a few minutes each evening writing about your day. Reflect on your achievements, challenges, and how you felt throughout the day. This process allows you to process your emotions and experiences, providing insight into your growth and areas for improvement. Journaling helps you understand yourself better and appreciate your journey, fostering a stronger sense of self-worth.

Acts of kindness are another way to enhance your self-worth. Each day, perform a small act of kindness, whether it's helping a colleague, complimenting a stranger, or volunteering your time. These acts not only benefit others but also provide you with a sense of purpose and fulfillment. Knowing that you can make a positive impact on others' lives reinforces your self-worth and the value you bring to the world.

Surround yourself with positive influences. Spend time with people who uplift and support you. Engage in activities and environments that make you feel good about yourself. Limit exposure to negative influences that drain your energy or make you doubt your worth. By curating your social and physical environments, you create a supportive network that reinforces your positive self-perception and self-worth.

Practice self-compassion daily. When you encounter setbacks or make mistakes, treat yourself with the same kindness and understanding you would offer a friend. Acknowledge your imperfections without harsh judgment. Self-compassion involves recognizing that everyone makes mistakes and that these do not define your worth. By being gentle with yourself, you foster a healthier relationship with yourself, which is crucial for sustained self-worth.

Develop a hobby or skill that you are passionate about. Dedicate time each day to engage in this activity. Whether it's painting, playing an instrument, cooking, or learning a new language, investing in something you love can bring joy and fulfillment. This practice allows you to express yourself and see tangible progress, which can boost your confidence and self-worth. Pursuing your interests reinforces the idea that your passions and talents are valuable and worth nurturing.

Limit your use of social media. While social media can be a great way to connect with others, it can also lead to comparisons and feelings of inadequacy. Set specific times for checking social media and be mindful of the content you consume. Follow accounts that inspire and uplift you, and unfollow those that make you feel less than. By managing your social media use, you protect your self-worth from the negative impacts of constant comparison.

Create a self -care ritual that you practice daily. This can include activities such as taking a relaxing bath, reading a book, practicing skincare, or simply spending quiet time alone. Self-care rituals are a way to show yourself love and respect, reinforcing the belief that you are worthy of care and attention. Consistently dedicating time to self-care can help you

feel more balanced and valued, which positively
impacts your self-worth.